Carl Kreider

1979

Dr. Orley R. Herron is president of the National College of Education in Evanston, Illinois. He is a past president of Greenville College and has served in key administrative positions at Indiana State University and the University of Mississippi. In addition to his doctorate, he holds an honorary Doctor of Letters degree from Houghton College. He is the author of numerous books and articles, including *The Role of the Trustee*, and *Input/Output* (Moody Press). Dr. Herron is married and has three children.

A CHRISTIAN EXECUTIVE in a SECULAR WORLD

A CHRISTIAN EXECUTIVE in a SECULAR WORLD

by

Orley R. Herron

THOMAS NELSON PUBLISHERS
Nashville New York

 Published in Nashville, Tennessee, by Thomas Nelson Inc., Publishers and simultaneously in Don Mills, Ontario, by Thomas Nelson & Sons (Canada) Limited. Manufactured in the United States of America.

Scripture verses marked KJV are from the King James Version of the Bible.
Scripture verses marked RSV are from the Revised Standard Version of the Bible, copyrighted 1946, 1952, © 1971, 1973.

ISBN 0–8407–5151–6

Ye are the salt of the earth: but if the salt have lost his savor, wherewith shall it be salted? it is thenceforth good for nothing, but to be cast out, and to be trodden under foot of men.

Ye are the light of the world. A city that is set on an hill cannot be hid. Neither do men light a candle, and put it under a bushel, but on a candlestick; and it giveth light unto all that are in the house. Let your light so shine before men, that they may see your good works, and glorify your Father which is in heaven.

—Matthew 5:13-16, KJV

Contents

Acknowledgments

A book never could be written without the help of many people. Sandy Larsen's unique skills were of outstanding assistance in drafting this manuscript. Without her the work would have been seriously delayed and perhaps never written. I salute her for her tremendous contribution.

Peter Gillquist's constant encouragement and editorial insights were of immeasurable value.

To my loving family—Donna, my devoted wife, Jill, Morgan, and Mark, our wonderful children—I give my eternal love. They kept me to the task of writing and with them I seek to model Christ-like leadership.

I wish to thank the class of 1951 of New Philadelphia, Ohio, who, with their advisors Mary Jane Hodder and Cy Williams, challenged me in those growing years to be the leader God was calling me to be. The friendship of members of that class continues until today.

For the staffs who have served me so ably over the years, I am grateful. For the hundreds of others who assisted along this journey, I am indeed thankful.

Evanston, Illinois
Fall, 1978

O.R.H.

Preface

For quite some time we have felt the need for a practical and straightforward book that would encourage male Christian executives in the secular world to be men of strength and integrity. We wanted a book that would encourage them to do things God's way in business even when the world's way seems easier and more fruitful.

Selecting the right author for such a book was all-important. It would have been relatively easy to find a godly pastor or the head of a Christian agency willing to mold biblical truths and his own ideas into a helpful volume. But, instead, we wanted to find a committed Christian involved directly in the arena of finance, decision making, head-to-head competition; someone who was victor, not victim, in the pressure-cooker atmosphere of the secular business world.

A CHRISTIAN EXECUTIVE IN A SECULAR WORLD

After nearly eighteen months, it came to our attention that an energetic, aggressive Christian man—one whose love for Christ was tastefully public—had accepted an appointment as president of the highly respected National College of Education on Chicago's suburban North Shore. Dr. Orley R. Herron, a young, middle-aged product of the mainline American evangelical movement, was making things happen at National College of Education.

But would a college president have the time to write? He'd *make* time, he said. Would he "tell it like it is" and give other Christian men the kind of *real* help and counsel they are looking for? You be the judge. In our opinion, he has done that and more.

—The Publisher

1

Who, Me?

Have you experienced this, too? You went ahead and got up, and all the rest of the day you were capable, knowledgeable, and aware. But for those first few seconds of the early morning, you were in a fog. You were out of town—certainly not home—but you didn't know where you were or why you were there.

Sift your memory now and tell me: Are there *other* times the same disorientation bumps up against you? As you step into your office, or as you're deep in a meeting with your associates, or as you scan your packed calendar, does the sensation nudge you? *I'm in the wrong place. Things are backward–blurred–I forget why I'm here. I'm not where I should be. I should be somewhere else.*

It's simpler to solve when you're traveling. Then the

answer's easy: *I don't feel at home because I am not at home; I am on a business trip*. The explanation is immediate, adequate, and satisfying.

But what about the other times? What about your flashes of odd unsettledness in the most familiar surroundings? They seem independent of the facts. After all, you know where you are. You like where you are. You're right where you worked for years to be. But then the unwanted question rudely tugs on your thoughts: *What in the world am I doing here?*

You're not alone. Moses, Gideon, and Jeremiah — each told by God to enter the secular world and have a liberating effect — all had the identical response: "*Who, me?*" To feel inadequate, ill-at-ease, and doubtful is certainly nothing new; a glance at those three people's lives shows that those feelings have been around for thousands of years.

You probably expect me to say that Christianity will ease your doubts, make you satisfied with life as it is. I am saying the opposite! A Christian executive, it seems to me, is even more prone to the sudden sensation of foreignness than is his non-Christian counterpart.

Why? Because a Christian who has any sensitivity realizes he is in God's service. Say that's you. You have a high sense of calling and duty. You remember that in the face of all your sins and failures, Christ forgave you and accepted you. You owe your Lord so much.

Your faith calls you to action. You should be attempting great things for God. You should be spreading the Word!

You look around. You see your desk: a city of paper-like skyscrapers. You see yourself placating both higher-ups and underlings. You endure endless meetings, and drag your eyes across interminable word-clogged reports. You are inescapably caught up in bitter business competition. You hear yourself saying what you must say to survive.

You are a phony, your head keeps saying. So you believe your head. You must be a fake. What does all *this* have to do with God? You are obviously in the wrong place.

You are falling short, then, and God is not pleased. You have to do something. Fast. Doesn't the Lord want you serving Him *fully?* Can't do that here! You don't have a spare minute. Your heart's divided. You're all bound up in profits, personnel, policy, promotions, PR. You can't point to anything anywhere that looks like service for God. Help!

It must be time to get out of this worldly work-harness and go full-time for the Lord. Find some Christian organization that needs your special talents. Management? Writing? Speaking? Finance? You're called upon to use those abilities for Christ, and for Christ only.

Devote yourself to Him completely, beckons your conscience. This is it; now's the hour. Go into full-time Christian service.

It's the only reasonable thing to do, isn't it? Your inner disturbance, your dissatisfaction—that must be the Holy Spirit telling you He wants more of you. Go ahead! Do it! Get into God's work. Get out of that strange place where you no longer fit.

Is that how you feel? If so, then I have something to share with you. It is something I have dug out of life with bone-weary fingers. It has tears on it, and more than a few battle scars. And it's for you, because I've thrashed about with those same uncertainties that are chipping away at your peace. Like you, I often have awakened in strange places.

I went from a Christian college to graduate school at a state university—then on to a position at another Christian college—then to two other state schools—then back into Christian education—then to a private secular institution. Time after time I woke up to the fact that the pillow was too hard and it was not my kind of art. Frequently the place looked strange. It felt like the *wrong* place. But then I remembered why I was there and what I had to do.

What I had to do—yes, that's the key—for years I was *mistaken* about what the Lord was actually calling me to do. I missed His quiet instructions in my own stumbling eagerness to serve Him well.

Plainly and simply, here's what I'm getting at: There is a call of God into the secular arena which is as real, clear, and significant as a call into the ministry. *You can experience the personal reign of Christ in a high-powered secular job.* It's true! And that's what this book is about. Specifically, we will look at:

- the process by which God brings a leader into positions of authority and responsibility;
- the human "gamble" inherent in stepping out to follow God's directions;
- the mistake of thinking that silk-smooth convenience and an easy road follow obedience;
- the satisfaction of life's pieces fitting together, ultimately, once we follow God's plan.

To do this, I will of necessity weave these lessons through the matrix of my own personal drama. Come back with me now to my first excitement of sensing my goal, my call—when I was thirteen.

2

Call Number 1

Today I don't panic when one of my kids looks a little bored in church, because I remember a night in First Baptist Church of New Philadelphia, Ohio, when I slumped back in the pew and stuck my legs out in front of me, primed (by habit) to be bored stiff.

The sermon was about to start. Again. Though I liked the special speaker—tall, good-looking Carl Burnham—I'd been listening to him every night for a week. I began to wonder why my friends in the Baptist Young People's Union had sat so far down in front.

My big brother, Niles, had let me wear his letter sweater, and its scratchy bulkiness felt like success. It was gold in color and on the front was a big black "P". For me, of course, high school was still two years away; but the warm sweater generated dreams of the days I'd earn my own letters at New Philadelphia High.

I fingered the blue-and-white spiral "Youth Sings," looked around, and my mind started to wander. . . .

High-ceiling Colonial church—full tonight, packed out. I've come to church here since forever; my mother teaches Sunday school. Carl talks on. He dresses nice. I like that tie. He's talking about two ways you can go. Ties are okay but I'd rather wear a black "P"!

Yeah, I know, heaven for good people, hell for the bad ones. No, that's not it, quite. Heaven for people who follow Christ and accept His mercy.

I flipped through the song book, then put it down beside me. We didn't sing my favorite that night.

I gotta listen to this guy. What's he saying? Jesus. The way out. No, not just the way out—the way in. *I get it. Carl makes it so clear. Christ pays—has* already *paid—for my wrongs, my sins. That's true? It must be! It makes sense. I can't earn God's love or rewards—can't earn my way to heaven.*

That night, as Carl Burnham explained, as my heart believed, Christ came to me. I knew I was forgiven for every wrong I'd done, and I knew I had a new life starting.

I was young. My insights weren't deep; my understanding wasn't refined. But I knew enough to know I was saved, a new Christian into whose life Jesus had come.

The next years were good ones. I was involved in sports, active in the church, and living and enjoying life to its fullest.

Our Baptist Young People's Union was a bubbling, busy

group, close-knit and yet concerned for outreach. We pooled our money and invaded local snack shops for sustenance. We practiced our music and went out to hold evangelistic meetings in children's homes, hospitals, and other churches, sometimes traveling seventy or eighty miles. The Baptist church broadcast a radio program five days a week, and often I was the soloist. I was elected BYPU president.

Each year in high school I was elected class president, too. Sports consumed my time and energies, and honors started coming my way. I co-captained the basketball and football teams and played trumpet in the band. I felt good about the way my life was going. God was smiling on me; no question about that.

Besides my other abilities, I was considered a budding young evangelist. My mother wrote the first sermon I ever preached. But I soon stepped out on my own and became the regular speaker at our BYPU outreach meetings. Billy Graham began his ministry about then, and he deeply inspired me; what better way to serve God, I reasoned, than by winning people to Christ?

The affirmations started coming: "Orley, you're going to be a preacher. God has His hand on you." I ate it up.

Our church supported missionaries to what was then the Belgian Congo, and when they came to speak, something in me stood up and walked in circles. A foreign assignment! Could the Lord have that in mind for me? My Christian life so far had been bright and successful and laden with potential. And now Africa, alive with mysteries, was beckoning. *I could come back and tell my own thrilling stories from that same pulpit,* I excitedly told myself.

Most important of all, it was what God *expected* of me. The half-hearted Christians worked at ordinary jobs; but for the dedicated, the totally sold-out, there was only one possible way to go. I'd heard it all my life. It had been drummed into me incessantly. The Lord *wants* us to serve Him full-time! You could choose either the pulpit or the mission field, but it had to be one or the other.

Could we do any less for Him? Of course not. Think what He'd done for us—His sacrifice, His self-denial, the completeness of His love. We owed Him everything.

Leave it for the fence-sitting Christians to live in two worlds; for us, the committed, the consecrated ones, it had to be all or nothing. We would surrender our secular aims and ambitions, and we'd give all our time for Christ. Hallelujah!

So at the altar I offered my life to God, pledging to serve Him as a missionary anywhere in the world. Hopefully, it would be Africa. But no matter where He might send me, I knew for sure that God had called me into His service. And that obviously meant becoming a preacher.

I loved to dance. As class president I had a hand in planning social events, and I thought they should involve *everybody;* high school social life shouldn't be only for the beautiful and popular and talented! I took some kids who had never learned to dance and taught them how. To say the least, I was an enthusiastic promoter of social dancing.

Then my church, the church in which I had been raised and had come to love Christ, switched denominations. We left the American Baptists to join up with the Conservative Baptists. Some attitudes that had begun changing were now solidified. The people sincerely believed that certain social practices hampered dedication to Christ, not the least of which was dancing.

Talk about a crisis in my young Christian life. I thought

dancing was a great thing; it gave kids a chance to get together and enjoy themselves. I didn't understand why it was wrong. I especially didn't understand how it could be right one day and wrong the next. When I thought about it, though, I realized that the people had simply changed their opinions. And, much as I hated to admit it, that was their right.

But what was *I* supposed to do? I couldn't change my opinion that easily. Everybody at school knew how much I liked dancing. Clearly, I was out on a limb.

Then in the middle of a basketball practice, gym-echoes in my ears and sweat in my eyes, puffing from exertion, I suddenly saw it: *When you're part of a team, you play the game by the rules.* Even if you think some rules are awkward or unnecessary, you go along with them if you want to participate. Of course, if you want to stage your own game, you can make up your own rules; but when you're on a team, you act like a part of the team.

So I made a decision: as long as I was involved in that church, whether I agreed with it totally or not, I would play by their rule book.

Just before my senior year, a young woman named Lydia Wire came from the Chicago area to serve our church as youth leader and organist. We loved her. The Lord shone from her life in an unmistakable way. The dynamism, creativity, and sheer intelligence of her faith deepened my own excitement about working full-time for God.

Lydia began talking to me about college. A Wheaton College graduate, she was convinced Wheaton was the place for me. I wasn't sure. My success in athletics had brought attractive scholarship offers. (My senior year we were undefeated in football, ranking sixth statewide, and our basketball team boasted the top scorer in Ohio.) My coaches wanted me to go to one of the state universities and play football.

I was tempted to follow their advice, but then how would I study for the ministry? Certainly a state school offered me no opportunities for preparing to serve the Lord! Maybe this was a test, I thought, to see how serious my commitment to the ministry was. If I meant what I said about becoming a preacher, I couldn't let the lure of secular success stop me.

Besides, there was another factor. Some of my friends in the church had stirred up self-doubts in me: They had pointed out that I often missed church activities because of school sports and the band. Was that right, they asked, to put outside interests first and give God my leftover time? How could I pretend I wanted to preach when the church was so unimportant to me?

I was stung. My young mind wrestled the question. I had decided to be a member of the church team and play by the rules; yet I would never have gotten that insight about "playing on the team" if I hadn't been involved in sports.

I didn't quit my school activities, but the doubts kept pestering me. Had I thoughtlessly alienated my Christian friends? Had I been unconsciously shortchanging the Lord? If my everyday life competed with God's work, how could I plan to enter the ministry?

Soon I'd be a grown-up, set in my ways. I wanted to be God's man; but if I followed Him, it had to be fully. He wanted me to enter His service, and I was going to do it.

In the fall of 1951, purposeful, idealistic, afraid, I went off to Wheaton College.

3

The Crisis of Change

"Orley, you should start planning a career in science."

"Huh?"

"Just look at your test scores," my advisor went on. "Science is where your aptitude lies. Have you thought about medicine? Organic chemistry? Research?"

I stumbled out of the office. Wheaton's trees and red-brick buildings blurred. All I could see was myself in the pulpit, scalpel in one hand and test tube in the other, wearing a long white lab coat, and sporting one of those head lamps, or whatever doctors wore.

No. The tests must be wrong. I was *already called!* I knew where my aptitude lay — in preaching. My place was the ministry. That's where I *belonged.*

I headed for my dorm, hunching my shoulders against the

fall chill. After all, would God give me gifts and then decide not to use them? If I could preach, then He wanted me to preach.

But then, if He also gave me aptitude in science, wouldn't He want to use that, too? Would He let *any* of my abilities go for naught?

What about sports? God hadn't forced me to give up sports. I'd already gone out for football; He was letting me use my athletic skill. I wasn't sure how it fit in with preaching, but I was enjoying it nevertheless.

But medicine? I kicked at a rock. Well, actually, if I let myself admit it, the thought had crossed my mind before. Niles and I had talked about it—I'd forgotten that until now. We had both talked about going into medicine. But I never took it all that seriously.

I glanced over at the chapel. They had good services there—not exactly like my home church, but that was okay. The music was great. There was plenty of musical talent in the student body.

Sometimes in chapel they had student speakers, good ones, too, some far better than I.

I squeezed sideways between two parked cars. *Most* people at Wheaton did things better than I did. Almost everybody was some kind of spiritual leader here. Who cares who was president of the BYPU in New Philadelphia, Ohio? Who cares who spoke at their outreach meetings or sang on the radio? Orley Herron? Who's he?

Maybe I shouldn't have come to Wheaton. I don't know what I'm doing here. Yes, of course I know—I'm studying to be a preacher. A preacher? Why? There are hundreds of good preachers. There of thousands of good preachers, and they are all going to school here at Wheaton College.

This is it. I'm leaving. I don't care if I've only been here for a week. Wheaton doesn't need me, and I sure don't need Wheaton. If I missed God's voice by *this* much—if I'm *this* far out of touch with God—I don't belong on any Christian college campus anywhere.

I could be playing ball right now at Ohio State and studying to be a doctor. Doctors make lots of money. Pro football players make lots of money. That's what I should have done—taken an athletic scholarship and gone on to greater things. Eventually I'd have been spotted by a scout for the Chicago Cardinals and been offered a juicy contract. Four years from now I could be in pro football—instead of off to a bare start in seminary.

Why had people told me over and over that I ought to be a preacher? Were they only looking at my speaking ability, my ease at meeting new people? Or were they more in tune with God than I was? I had preached; people had responded; people had actually come to faith in Christ through the outreach meetings I led. But what did that prove?

Was it my fruitfulness, or the church's enthusiastic approval of my fruitfulness, that pushed me toward the pulpit?

I opened the door to Unit I dorm, plain and institutional, laced with bowling-alley halls — my nearest thing to home in Wheaton. The stairs rumbled and two fellows who passed me barked a greeting: "Orley! How ya doin'?"

I started up the steps. The hallway felt oppressively warm. I shifted my books to the other arm.

If God *had* called me, how could I not respond? Forget that others He called might have more skills; forget that idea of becoming a doctor or of playing pro ball.

Of course! Regardless of what else I could do with my talents, God wanted me to work for Him, and He'd promised to find a place for me.

I unlocked my door and pushed it open. Home. I tossed

my books down on the bed and sprawled alongside them.

What a relief! At long last, the issue was settled. I would obey God's will and become a preacher.

For months I had noticed a tall, self-assured man striding about the campus. He was Glenn Heck, principal of Wheaton Junior High, and a part-time instructor on the college education faculty. My path crossed Prof. Heck's more and more often, and we became acquainted. He seemed to know where he was going, confident that life held the best for him. I wondered why he wasn't a minister.

In a friendly turn of events, David Burnham became my roommate during my sophomore year. It was his father, Carl, whose preaching had led me to Jesus Christ.

Dave and I both became close to the Hecks, and at the start of our junior year, we took a room in Glenn and Ginnie's newly built home. At about the same time, our combined impulsiveness prompted a meeting that rearranged my life.

I had been dating various girls, both at Wheaton and back home over the summers. A few times I had thought of getting serious about somebody, but nothing ever quite worked out. My relationships frequently fizzled, even though I had little trouble getting dates. If I tried to come across as the fun type, my date preferred someone profound. If I tried to be profound, she asked me why I was gloomy. My "great evangelist" dream was a super-pious sop to some, but if I tried to offseffset it by acting frivolous, the girls wondered if there was a serious side to me at all.

At football camp the week before the start of my junior year, I began to dread going back to more of the same. Fed up, I looked to God to get me out of my romantic swamp. "Lord," I said, "I'm goofing up all my efforts at dating. I don't even know what a good relationship is, or how to find it. I mean, how to find *her.* So I'm not going to date another person unless You show me—unless I know it's Your leading."

It was a nervy, impulsive prayer, but I meant it. I'm sure I never gave God the option of my embracing celibacy. I simply hoped He would do a better job of matchmaking than I had done so far.

A week later, microphone cords snaking across the gym floor and pep-rally echoes rebounding, the Wheaton football team was introduced to the student body. My heroic daydreams were crudely cut off by my roommate's thumb in my ribs.

"Orley! See that girl over there? I'm asking her out tonight." I looked toward the person Dave pointed out and announced, "I'm asking the one sitting next to her."

Then I remembered my prayer! Had it melted? Evaporated? Well, God had let the words come out of my mouth, hadn't He? At the close of the pep rally I walked across the gym and met Donna Morgan, the freshman from Oregon whose lovely eyes and ready smile had attracted me.

When Donna and I took a walk together that night, I felt certain that I would marry her. Here was the girl I would come to love. On our second date, I kissed her. Though we weren't formally engaged until two years later, and though we both went out with other people, I could not quiet the persistent inner voice saying Donna was the one for me.

Fortunately my new love did not balk at the idea of marrying a preacher. My major in history would let me continue my ministerial studies at Wheaton's graduate school; from a B.D. program I altered my course to a Master's in biblical literature. My time away from studying was taken up with being men's head resident, leading the youth group at

River Forest Presbyterian Church, coaching the ends for Wheaton's football team—and Donna.

We were married on August 24, 1956, a wedding date partly dictated by my counseling at a summer camp that ended only a few days earlier. I hurried to Portland and participated in the most beautiful wedding ever—not because of the details (most of which I've forgotten) but because of my beautiful bride.

In September we returned to Wheaton and set up housekeeping in a residence-hall apartment. Donna had one more year before graduation; I was still pursuing my Master's.

With room in my schedule for some electives, I snapped up a professor's suggestion that I take an education course or two. I was fascinated!

The counseling angle especially intrigued me. What satisfaction there would be in helping people escape from their trapped lives so they might enjoy the freedom that lies in Christ!

I knew now that pastoral counseling would be an important part of my ministry. And I was going to be a minister. That much was certain.

Increasingly I wondered why Glenn, such a clear example of a man who lived in God's presence, had chosen an occupation several steps down from the pulpit. Surely God had called *him*. Then he must be running from God! No, living in the same house day after day, I had seen that Glenn was not running from anything; he was relaxed, open, and certain he was in the right place.

Of course there *was* a need for Christian teachers, that was obvious; after all, Wheaton College wouldn't have existed without them. Yet, teachers stood somewhere below pastors in the Lord's hierarchy of service, didn't they?

Or did they? The more college experience I gained, the flimsier that premise looked. Who had told me pastors were the top of the pyramid? Where had I gotten that idea? I couldn't pin down its source. But I couldn't remember ever *not* believing it.

Everyone in my home church thought preachers were the pinnacle of Christian commitment; at least, that was what had been communicated to me. They had told me I should become a pastor *because* I was gifted; in other words, ministers were supposed to be the most gifted people. Ministers did not merely exercise special, unique gifts; they were *more gifted* than the laity—or so I had interpreted what I'd been told.

Perhaps I had misunderstood those people. Or perhaps they had been wrong. At any rate, across my months and years at Wheaton, the bulldog belief that serving God meant standing in the pulpit began to ease its grip. An odd and startling relief came washing over me.

Why was I relieved? Didn't I *want* to be a preacher? Was I trying to escape? Squirm out of it?

Maybe relief was a danger signal! Maybe my spiritual life was getting slack. God had called me, and I had to follow His call, *whether or not* the ministry was the highest order of service.

Yes, even if the pulpit turned out to be the *lowest* place, that was still where I belonged, because that was where Jesus had called me—wasn't it? I wanted Him to run my life and take care of my future, and very deeply I wanted to occupy the place He had for me. I wanted to bring His message to people, to minister to people just as Carl Burnham had ministered to me. And as Ralph Raymond (the pastor who'd come when we changed denominations) and Glenn Heck had ministered to me.

But *Glenn wasn't a minister.* The simple thought jerked hard on my insides. Glenn *wasn't* a minister. Yet he had ministered to me; there was no denying that. I was closer to God, I was more aware of others, I knew myself better because of his influenceence on my life. And he had been ministering—in his classroom and in his home, without benefit of ordination.

A study of faith and the miracles in John's Gospel would make up my Master's thesis. The passages on which I drilled were words I had read hundreds of times before, always with attention to the miraculous acts themselves. I had thought the accounts were there only to prove Jesus' divinity and to demonstrate His good works.

Now, because of my educational training, I focused for the first time on the *learners*—the followers who saw their Teacher do these wonders. What lessons had they reaped from Jesus' actions? Had they *changed* because they saw His miracles?

I was amazed—though I should have known better—at their dullness, unbelief, doubts. How could they have been so thick-headed? Sprinkled among the sweet nuggets of the miracles, like sand in candy, was the constant skepticism of the people closest to Christ.

"They did not understand what He was saying to them . . . . His disciples did not understand this at first . . . . 'What sign do you do, that we may see, and believe you?' . . . . 'What are five loaves and two fish among so many?' . . . 'How can this be?' . . . 'This is a hard saying; who can listen to it?' . . . 'Unless I see in his hands the print of the nails, and place my finger in the mark of the nails, and place my hand in his side, I will not believe". . . . on and on it went. Hadn't they been listening? Learning? Observing?

Why was simple faith always *beyond* these people? Why did they ask so many questions?

Why did *I* ask so many questions? From that angle, my record was no better than theirs! I looked back over my college days and recalled a stream of personal uncertainty—dilemmas—ponderings—*questions*. The Lord must be as impatient with me as He'd been with His faithless disciples.

Shaken, I looked again at the Bible. And again I was surprised that I'd read the words so often, yet missed this simple truth: Jesus didn't scold and reprimand His followers so much as He stopped and *explained* to them. He resolved their confusion as well as He could, supplying just as many answers as they could absorb. And then He said, "Follow me. Keep on following me."

Perhaps Christ hadn't condoned all people's doubts, but neither had He rejected all their wonderings. He talked to the doubters and helped them learn trust. He reminded them of the miracles they'd seen. He interpreted His own words. He encouraged the small-faithed. He showed them His hands and His side.

Thus, Christianity holds plenty of opportunity for queries, I reasoned, as long as we sincerely want the truth—*as long as we wait for the Lord's response* and don't arrogantly withdraw after asking.

To raise a question is to expect a reply; to walk off afterwards is to say there is no answer. "Will you also go away?" Christ sadly asked the twelve, after others had abandoned Him. He wanted them to stay (doubts and all) and hear Him in more depth.

For the first time I saw it: Problems are *part* of a healthy, robust faith! Where else can learning start? How else can we grow? What teacher wants to face a class that never asks a question?

Teacher . . . the word stirred something in me. Of course! That was what I wanted to be! Over the months the Lord had been shifting my interest gears, and now teaching held far more appeal for me than pastoring.

Had God changed His mind about me? I couldn't live believing that God was capricious, training me for one job and then shoving me into something else. Had my recurring doubts about preaching been justified? What was going on?

One thing I knew *was* happening: I now felt comfortable about going into education and uncomfortable about the ministry.

I thoroughly believed God was guiding me through my new inclinations. Alongside the certainty of His leading, another sure thing was this: If I was serious about education, it meant our transferring to another school. I began investigating some possibilities, and over the months kept coming back to the same one—Michigan State University at Lansing. MSU had a solid nationwide reputation in student-services training, and I liked what I heard and saw of the school.

But did I like it enough to bend the direction of all my plans and studies so far? Since that revival night in the New Philadelphia Baptist Church, my whole life had been rushing headlong for the pulpit. If I suddenly darted off course, who could say where I might wind up? There was no telling.

I got out my Bible and looked at the lives of some other people whose lives had been changed in mid-course. David was happily herding sheep when Samuel called him in to anoint him king of Israel—what a shock that must have been! And Saul, David's predecessor, had to be brought out of hiding when the time came for him to become king—the prospects of new responsibility were scary. Nehemiah was cupbearer to the king before God called him to be general contractor for rebuilding Zion's wall. Saul, who had violently persecuted the church, met Christ in an encounter that revolutionized his life; his new name, Paul, symbolized his new identity.

So I knew I wasn't alone in facing transformation. That was a comfort; yet it still didn't answer the question of what we should do in our particular case.

Should we go to Lansing? It would mean changing everything. My new bride and I were living in the dorm as house parents, paying thirty-five dollars a month for our two-bedroom apartment. Donna had landed a job teaching kindergarten after her graduation; she would have to give up her teaching job. I was in my third year of graduate study, hard at work on a Master's thesis for a degree I would never earn; it would mean beginning my graduate studies all over again. And it would mean revising who I thought I was.

Most nagging, most pestering to me, it would mean having to *explain* to all those people why I wasn't going into the ministry.

4

Getting to Know the Other World

We were crazy about Lansing. That shouldn't have surprised us; we had followed the Lord there in trust and good faith.

It wasn't our financial security making us happy! We barely knew what that was. Blessedly, Donna was again hired to teach kindergarten, and later I found a part-time job in Knapps Clothing Store selling suits. The certainty of God's purpose for us gave us peace even in our student poverty.

Donna was confident we'd made a wise move. In college she'd encountered the stream of people who for some reason always poured out their problems to me. She had felt even then that student work would be the ideal career for me.

Not everyone else saw it that way. My expectations came true: People wrote and asked me what on earth I thought I was doing. Hadn't God's call to me been clear?

Yes, God's call was very clear, clearer than ever before. We discovered that (despite the opinions of others) we could move ourselves and our situation *without* moving outside His will. Every day I felt life widening all around me, making room for what I was going to be. I wanted to dance a jig across campus!

MSU believed in developing people to do their jobs well. My field, technically "administrative and educational services," encompassed many down-to-earth methods for helping university students grow.

Some of my spiritual stereotypes began to shatter. Even without a working knowledge of biblical love, the MSU faculty cared deeply about making student life meaningful. They wanted to open up ways for young adults to cope better, to handle the pressures of relationships and studies, and the future, without folding.

I had thought of the secular world's approach to life only as ignorance's poor substitute for the Christian way. Now I was surprised to find students and educators "out there" with many aims identical to the Christian's. Through God, I knew the very qualities they sought to produce in people *could happen*. My finding a position in college administration would mean wide influence for Christ—working with people who were already out to improve themselves, showing the life-transforming effects the Lord could have.

At Christmastime that first year, I became head resident for Shaw Hall East with a dozen resident assistants working under me. The stately older residence hall housed 750 students, each one filled to bursting with life and promise.

Donna and I were attending Trinity Church in East Lansing, pastored by Eugene Williams and made up largely of university people. There was an active church basketball league in the area, and since I knew several other head residents who wanted to play basketball, I helped organize a team. It was partly a crafty way to get MSU staff members to come to church. By league rules players were required to attend a certain number of services per month! We even won the church league championship.

As the long, gray Michigan winter eased into spring, we met a university phenomenon of which we'd been previously innocent— the panty raid. An excess of nervous energy had been brewing in our halls for several weeks.

The thick snow was vanishing, revealing welcome patches of green. And then it happened. One warm spring night the men's dorms were suddenly vacant. A mass of male shadows flowed across the lawn toward the women's dorms. The head residents made a facsimile of riding herd; I was probably the only one who didn't know what was about to break loose.

The girls were obviously prepared. Shrieks, laughs, and underwear rained down from their windows, an absurd scene that shattered all the tensions of the winter. After my first shock, the sight amused me. Just as I was wondering if this could ever happen at Wheaton, a flash of orange light stabbed my eyes.

Somebody had set some trash on fire. I heard glass break. My defenses went up—against what, I didn't know. I had seen or kicked an inordinate number of beer bottles on the grass, and I knew energies were at full tide. More glass. Suddenly a body collided with mine, then ran into the night as I regained my balance.

Then I tuned in to it—the crowd noise was building fast. Soon, more ominous sounds of defiance drowned out the frivolous giggles. I couldn't hear what people were saying, but the roar was rising, deepening. Two shadows appeared to scuffle. Was that another fire I glimpsed, farther off? I heard a sharp cry of pain.

It was like a movie. A lynch mob in the wild west. But this wasn't a movie. This was happening—here, to me, to MSU, to my campus. I felt myself groping for a button to shut it all off. I was powerless.

I should get out of here and let it run its course. They'd calm down eventually. Things would be okay. People can stay mad only so long. Besides, they weren't *really* that mad; it was mostly just a joke, wasn't it?

Unfortunately, it wasn't a joke. What began as student frivolity turned into mob violence. State police were called in to quell the disturbance, the first of three times during our years at MSU that state lawmen moved in to control a panty-raid-turned-riot.

What we didn't know then, of course, was that these disturbances were signals of student unrest that would be unleashed in full force during the Vietnam war years.

I learned one important basic from those days of campus upheaval: that though negotiation is necessary, negotiation cannot take place in chaos. Before the two sides (or three, or four) can talk, order must be restored—not brutally, for that only adds to violence. Indeed, tolerance and understanding are in the spirit of Christ; anarchy is not.

We had happier experiences at MSU, of course! With feet in both the student world and the staff world, Donna and I enjoyed the privileges of both. We went to the football games and activities, helped map out Shaw's social schedule, ate with the kids, and listened to their problems and dreams.

I wanted my staff to hear the message of Christ from

powerful Christian speakers who would stimulate later bull sessions, opening more opportunities for us to talk about our faith. We were able to secure several collegiate speakers who explained how one could enter into a personal relationship with Jesus Christ. The talks stirred up curiosity; a number of people later came to us with questions. Besides giving us the chance to offer spiritual help, the encounters sharpened my counseling techniques.

My formal counseling internship was pure practical experience. I was put into very real situations: People came to my small office, and I put all my skill and sensitivity to work helping them deal with their problems. But my counselee and I were not alone. Through a microphone in the telephone, my supervisor listened to the conversation and later offered his criticisms. The "subject" knew of the eavesdropping—though I wondered sometimes which one of us was the subject.

In December of 1959, barely before New Year's, Shaw Hall East added a tiny new resident, our daughter Jill. In my rush to tell our relatives the good news, I tried to telegram: "JILL DONNETTE HAS ARRIVED. MOTHER AND DAUGHTER DOING FINE." Weeks later I discovered that my hastily dictated message actually read: "DILL DOUGHNUT ARRIVED. MOTHER AND DAUGHTER DOING FINE."

My level of communication ought to have been higher, since by this time I was working on a Ph.D. The dissertation subject would be the teaching of religion at colleges and universities; course work would be completed shortly. Donna and I, now parents, had to look ahead to the time our student life would be over.

As we asked the Lord for the wisdom to choose right, we saw the crux of the decision forming: It was going to be education, but would it be a secular environment or a Christian environment?

Michigan State had baptized me into wideness. At Lansing I'd learned the startling, liberating truth that God was free to *not* work in ways I expected. I learned He could shake off the methods I had labeled "standard procedure" and do what He wanted, when He pleased.

Still, our hearts went back to Wheaton days. There'd been an atmosphere of love there, a bond of understanding between us and others who loved Christ. To serve at a Christian school meant going back to a community of people who shared deepest purposes with us. And, after all, we craved a safe environment for Jill.

But (why did a "*but*" always and forever jump up to ambush my reasoning?) we didn't want Jill raised in a closed, contained atmosphere. My own background had wrapped me in a narrowness I was only now beginning to shed. In a purebred Christian community, would the same thing happen to her? We wanted her safe; we did not want her stifled.

At Wheaton I had realized I didn't have to be a *pastor* to be a servant of Christ; maybe now I was facing the same question in a different form. I hadn't required a "holy" profession to do my best work for the Lord; did I now need a "holy" place? Of course not. Besides, the only jobs being offered me were positions at state universities.

Michigan State's administrative training program was famous, and its graduates were sought-after and highly placed. Dean of Students, Dean of Men, Vice President for Student Affairs, Director of Student Personnel—the offers looked tempting. All from secular schools. Not one from a Christian college. Then God's leading was obvious! Or—was it?

Reluctantly I took another look at my desires: I wasn't

nearly as *willing* to go to a Christian school as I liked to think. In fact I was hoping God wouldn't call us to one, hoping my lack of interest was from Him. I was afraid that serving at a Christian college, for all its love and support, might entangle me again in trivialities.

When you're part of a team, you play by the rules; I still believed in the principle. Therefore, on a Christian campus I'd have to fit myself to whatever bias surrounded me; and I didn't think I was ready to be driven back into rigidness.

I didn't want to turn into a "born-again complainer" who grumbled at any challenge to his faith, resisting the encounters the Lord brought into his life. I didn't want to hide away in some religious ghetto where there was little opportunity to reach out naturally to unbelievers. There were pressures at Lansing, but they were the price we'd paid to be the salt of the earth and the light of the world—in our corner of it.

Life was more *exciting* at a state university! There were simply more ideas around, a variety of people with varying lifestyles, and more things to do. We actually *enjoyed* our unbelieving friends at MSU. We were challenged by knowing people who didn't think as we thought.

Not that we went along with all our university associates in everything; we didn't always buy their morals, their humanism, their outlook on life, or their opinions of God. Donna and I had tried to maintain a clear witness for Christ, resisting any ideas we thought were false.

But if our stand had consistently been for the truth of Christianity—then we'd been in conflict with the philosophy of teamwork at MSU! We had often gone against prevailing opinions. We hadn't accepted the worldly viewpoints of the people we worked with.

What had changed? For years I'd trusted my insight on

"teamwork" that had come during a high school basketball practice. Now I found I wasn't living by it! I wondered why.

The answer wasn't long in coming: There'd been a flaw in my original thought. Being part of a team means playing by the rules—not the rules *of the team*, but the rules of the *sport itself*. Now, finally, I was not playing anyone's game but God's. The team was no longer of first importance to me.

I shared this with Donna, and she smiled knowingly; it was a truth she'd come upon long ago. Donna walked with the Lord, unaffected by other people's opinions and expectations. She knew that whether others accepted her or not, Christ accepted her, and that was the secret of her relaxed radiance. Now I was beginning to make it my own.

We *could* work at a Christian college, then, enjoying the good things of its atmosphere and giving ourselves to its people, without being smothered by any artificial regulations. We were free to be ourselves, regardless of who the people around us were. Still the fact remained that no Christian school had invited me to join its staff.

"Lord, we're willing to serve You wherever you want, in education of any kind, any place. Please let us know what our future should be, and we'll follow You," was our fervent prayer.

Together Donna and I opened ourselves to all God's possibilities. Of course, at the time, there on my knees, my willingness to accept nonexistent offers from Christian schools seemed like a safe enough bet.

I was wrong. In the next few days six Christian colleges wrote me, offering identical jobs.

5

The God Who Shows Up

So Donna and I snapped up one of those offers, packed up, moved, and have stayed there ever since—right?

Well, not exactly.

Our decision to go to Westmont College was nearly instantaneous; only six weeks after our prayer, as my plane landed at the airport in Santa Barbara, California, I was overcome by the certainty that here was the place for us. The interviews only confirmed my first impression. I was hired as Dean of Students for the lovely, garden-decked college in the Santa Ynez foothills above the Pacific.

If Westmont's idyllic setting lulled us toward tranquility, the student mood quickly woke us up. Westmont kids were inquisitive and refused to swallow the easy answers. After our free-wheeling MSU experience, we appreciated their unrestricted spirit.

The years in California soon proved to be our best ones yet. We had the peace and good feeling that come naturally when people do what they like to do. Of course we knew the contentment came from God. That was how He had always worked with us, confirming His will by our internal happiness.

And we were certainly happy in Santa Barbara. Two more children were born to us there: dark-haired Morgan and blond, blue-eyed Mark. Southern California living suited us perfectly: relaxed and easy, yet vibrant and fresh. The Santa Barbara climate was like heaven; so was the wild, lush, rocky scenery.

For a while we lived in a rented house, then moved to an apartment in the new Van Kampen residence hall. But our family was expanding rapidly, and it was obvious we would soon outgrow the apartment. We held our breaths and took the plunge into buying a home of our own.

The big, open house we found and purchased epitomized California living—indoors flowing into balmy outdoors—and it was only a block from campus. Students and faculty came by, sharing burdens, plans, and prayers with us. It was good to be back where believers made up the majority.

Our years in Santa Barbara spanned most of the sixties; the times weren't easy for young people on any campus, including Westmont. The early counterculture was flourishing almost literally in our back yard.

Above us in the mountains lived about ninety "families" of sun-worshipers. Many went naked. The men wore their hair long (unheard of at the time) and they saluted the brilliant Pacific sunsets by firing off a cannon. We called them the Sundowners. For communication between homes they flew coded flags; the bright banners flapping in the California sun seemed to herald a siege on tradition.

Westmont kids, never blasé about academics, were no more blasé about blind acceptance of authority. The school paper *Horizon* began deftly chipping away at college policy. Disputed issues varied in weightiness, and so did the students' grounds for criticism. But I felt their questioning was sincere.

With interest I watched the response of my fellow administrators and faculty. Some were threatened by student outspokenness, others threw in their lot with the campus radicals, still others stayed quietly tolerant and hoped the whole thing would go away. My MSU experience had stuck with me, so my own feelings were mixed.

I was sure of one thing: Communication lines had to be kept wide open. Students were obviously dissatisfied, and ignoring their dissatisfaction would only hurt and frustrate them further. If the college was being faulted, I was determined at least that one fault would *not* be the administration's refusal to listen. These young, thinking adults were telling us something; we had to be adult enough to open our ears. And *they* had to be adult enough to listen to us in return.

Looking back, the issues seem trivial now. There was a rule against beards; six students started growing them. Some of the trustees thought the whiskers spelled conformity to worldly fashions and ideas. I couldn't see what difference it made. The Bible clearly stated that man looks on the outside, but God looks on the inside, judging us by our hearts rather than our faces. The students kept their beards, and, having made their point, shaved them off immediately after commencement!

Several of Westmont's rules struck me as unreasonably strict. Freshman women had to be in by 7 P.M. on week nights, and freshmen were not allowed cars. According to research I had seen at Michigan State, cars and later hours were not very detrimental to the academic growth of students serious about college. I challenged the rules and eventually saw them eased.

The regulations had not been set up blindly; they were there to prevent students from misusing certain things by making those things entirely unavailable. The intent was good. Yet I questioned the wisdom of such an "absolute no" method.

How could a young person learn to handle something if he was never exposed to it? Sheltering him completely was treating him like a child, not like a decision-making adult. His morals had to be in his heart; if they weren't, if they were only imposed from outside, he would leave them with us after graduation along with his cap and gown and gym suit.

The encounters were painful. Time after time at student council meetings I found myself put through the mill, working to defend our administrative decisions while staying open to student ideas. I left the meetings drained, yet oddly exhilarated that Westmont was producing people who could *think*.

These kids hadn't needed to go somewhere else to exercise their minds. We were growing a crop of young Christians who tackled the tough questions, and we were being sharpened in return. Now, far removed from the situation, I can see how student-faculty differences actually fed free thought. We excited each other.

On a hot, dry day the administration was meeting in President Roger Voskuyl's office when there was a rapping on the door. Dr. Ed Bouslough leaned in and said the words every Southern Californian dreads: "There's a fire!"

We hurried outside. About a quarter of a mile away, up on Mountain Drive where the Sundowners lived, we spotted a small blaze. It looked like a harmless little bonfire, but no fire was harmless in this part of the country. Here, it could mean annihilation. Vegetation was very dry, and the hot "devil winds" coming down the mountain could pick up burning pieces of wood and shoot them like flaming arrows.

We alerted head residents in the dorms to be ready to

evacuate, though I didn't expect the blaze to be all that serious. By nightfall, however, fifteen hundred firefighters swarmed the campus, and by the next day there were three thousand.

The air was glutted with smoke, choking us, blinding us. We asked any students with firefighting experience to stay. We told the rest to wrap all they could in sheets and get out.

Fire or no fire, we had to chuckle at that preposterous parade of young hoboes laden with their lumpy, bulging sheets. They packed off to gymnasiums, churches, homes, wherever they could go. We stayed and fought the fire.

We were numbed to learn of an awful mistake: The couplings on our fire hoses did not match the hydrants on campus. There was only one that fit and was usable. With every truck and hose for miles around already in service, we could hardly go borrowing equipment.

Sadly, a single fire hose was no match for the onrushing flames. We were losing. The fire reached the college, taunting us like a thousand Goliaths, while we stood clutching barely one sling. It was all unfair! Had God abandoned Westmont, after everything He'd done to help us? Was He going to let it be incinerated? Had He forgotten?

The cruelty of the hose-coupling fiasco hit us harder as we saw the monster advancing, eating trees and houses like they were popcorn. Five spots on the campus were burning now. We wept. But the firefighters kept working—an army of tireless, brave men. *They* hadn't given up, though Westmont College meant nothing to them. Where was our faith?

At least I knew Donna and the children were safe. They had left the house and gone to a friend's, taking only the baby books and some photographs.

The mayor of Santa Barbara came. I told him we would lose the campus if we didn't get more help. He understood, he said, but most of the trucks were caught in a backfire on the mountain and couldn't get out. As the mayor's car pulled away, it looked like the end for us.

We'd been awake for two solid days. Nightfall had come the second time, but the sky was a terrifying orange. I stood gasping for air. The field just above our main administration building was in flames; Catherwood residence hall, a lovely old estate, was burning down.

I could see it was over. It was time to leave, evacuate, get all human life out of there and let the buildings go. Every nerve and bone of my body ached for rest. If we could get out, get far enough from the fire, get a safe distance from here, I could sleep. That was all I wanted now. Let it all burn, and I'll just sleep. Sleep. Sleep . . . .

Good grief, I'm hallucinating. I'm so tired, I'm going crazy. Out of the bitter solid-black smoke burst a gleaming white fire truck. *There's no such thing as a white fire truck. It's an angel. I'm no longer here.*

I took a deep breath, expecting the air of heaven, and nearly coughed my lungs out. The smoke was still real. Then the fire truck was real, too!

I ran to it on strength that came from somewhere, and was met with a shouted question from the driver: "Where's the turnoff to the fire camp?"

"We need you here!" I shouted back. "Do your couplings fit these hydrants?"

I never thought watching a hose go onto a fire hydrant could cause me bliss. With that one truck they beat back the fire and Westmont College was saved!

We laughed and celebrated and thanked the Lord over and over for His sending the white angel. Later we learned that the firemen had come from Los Angeles, a hundred miles away, missed a turnoff and pulled up at the college to ask directions. I had never seen before, nor have I seen since, another white fire truck.

The heavy atmosphere at Westmont cleared away along with the smoke from the forest fire. Students, faculty, and administration had cooperated to evacuate the campus and save property and lives. I believe now (though it never crossed my mind in the heat and fumes of the battle) that the hand of the Lord was in that fire, to show us how much we needed each other. Tensions were eased and a new spirit of love literally rose from the ashes.

God showed up just when we doubted He was there or that He cared! Of course He was there all along; but we needed to be made more sensitive to Him—and to one another. He saved the campus physically; but even more than that, He saved it spiritually. Barriers melted in the flames.

Soon Donna and I, faced with questions about my doctorate and our future, would personally need a God who "shows up."

When I left Michigan State, I still needed to complete foreign language and dissertation requirements before receiving my Ph.D. In fact Donna and Jill had moved to Santa Barbara without me, while I remained in Lansing for the summer struggling to study French—not very successfully.

Over the years at Westmont I became aware of the power held by college and university boards of trustees. Although 34,000 trustees nationwide controlled student life for millions, many of them looked on colleges as businesses and lacked thorough knowledge or close personal interest in education.

The more I thought about and studied the phenomenon,

the greater my interest grew, until finally I abandoned my previous dissertation plans and began collecting data for a dissertation about in-service training programs for boards of trustees.

Believe it or not, the dissertation was actually fun. I enjoyed the entire process. And the time wore wings. After collecting material for a year, I wrote for five solid, intense weeks, all day every day except Sunday. At the end of the time I got down on my knees and thanked the Lord for His constant help. I could hardly believe the writing had gone so swiftly.

French, however, was still staring me in the face—uncompleted, incomprehensible French. I simply had not made the grade at Lansing and had not been motivated to continue my efforts in Santa Barbara. Foreign languages weren't my favorite field of study. In fact only one language course had ever excited me: *koine* Greek, the language of the New Testament, back at Wheaton.

That was it! Write MSU about the Greek I'd had at Wheaton! But no, I remembered hearing that Michigan State never accepted biblical Greek to fulfill a language requirement, since it was possible to fake it by memorizing New Testament passages. Still, it was worth a try.

I wrote to the MSU dean, feeling not at all like the fellow dean I was. A stab of undergraduate vulnerability hit me—fresh sympathy for our students and for all students whose futures hung on administrative decisions they could not control.

The answer came amazingly soon, and what an answer—to prayer! My three years of *koine* Greek at Wheaton fulfilled the language requirement for the Ph.D. We were delirious with joy! Except for minor changes in the dissertation demanded by my committee, nothing now stood between me and my degree.

6

Not Knowing Is Sometimes Normal

". . . he went out, not knowing whither he went (Heb. 11:8, KJV)."

That was fine for Abraham, but surely those words would never apply to *me!* I'd always believed a spiritual person knew where he was headed; he had a goal, a clear idea of God's plan for his life, and a sanctified strategy for getting there.

Abraham? Well, certainly the Lord had called him to move to an unknown land. But that must have been a special case.

Toward the end of our time at Westmont College, I began to think the opposite might be true: The unspiritual man needs to know what's going on so he can take care of himself; the man of faith can afford to be adventuresome, since He trusts God to lead him to a good land. Sure enough, the Lord took me up on my insight.

Whether it was the winning of the long-sought doctorate, Westmont's sailing through a stiff accreditation test, the completion of our family, or the simple voice of God, I did not know.

At any rate, I began to feel restless at Santa Barbara. For me the place was still wide enough. Yet, starting to nag me was the hollow sensation that my work there was over. Nothing threatened my position. No one was after my job. I merely felt I should move on, and the feeling would not go away.

"The wind bloweth where it listeth," Jesus had said, "and thou hearest the sound thereof, but canst not tell whence it cometh, and whither it goeth: so is every one that is born of the Spirit (John 3:8, KJV)." Who are we to pick, choose, and predict where the Holy Spirit will send us next?

Donna was willing to go but saw some difficulties. Although Jill, Morgan, and Mark were too small to have much say in the matter, she was concerned about their trauma in being uprooted without knowing why.

Much later I would discover how Donna's view of change balances and softens mine. I see the challenge and charge ahead; Donna wisely sees the risks and weighs the circumstances. My view is usually: "Let's throw the 'big bomb' in the fourth quarter and try to win it all!" Donna might choose to protect a 21-21 tie.

Like a steam locomotive, I can get fired up and lurch away from the station without looking back to see if all the cars are hooked together. Ten miles down the track I check and find out I'm running all alone. Decisiveness is fine; but a decisive leader can also be an isolationist, insensitive to the people around him in their personal pain of change.

For now, in our situation at Westmont, since confusion

clouded our lives, I did the only thing I knew to do: I looked for the shortest route out of our confusion.

Job offers had come my way, but I'd been paying them small attention because we felt settled in Santa Barbara and liked our life there. Now I examined one possibility more closely: a position at the University of Mississippi at Oxford. Ole Miss was giving me the chance to direct their doctoral program in student personnel work—in other words, teaching people to do what I was already doing.

The opportunity looked better as I thought more about it. The experience and training I'd gotten on-the-job at Westmont would pay off for other potential deans of students. Leaving the Christian support of Westmont would be a blow, but I knew that the dean of the Ole Miss school of education was a believer. Our friends in Santa Barbara were sad but understanding. Some tried to talk us into staying, then eased off when they saw our decision was firm.

Though I'd been born in Kentucky, my family had moved to Ohio when I was a baby so I'd never actually lived in the South. On the red clay of Mississippi we stood out as imports and Yankees. Yet authentic Southern kindness abounded.

Donna will never forget the day, during the long discouragement of our search for housing, when a tire blew out as she was driving from Memphis to Oxford all alone. As she sat by the highway, crying in frustration, some workmen mowing grass came over and cheerfully changed the tire for her.

Among the small town's limited rentals we finally found a dreary two-bedroom apartment; our kids shared a towering triple bunk bed. Later, through a good friend who managed the U.S. Plywood plant, we learned of an unexpected treasure: A

Florida college president's red brick house, built in Oxford for his future retirement, stood vacant and was now for rent. We took it gleefully. It was on a huge wooded lot; I counted more than a hundred trees one day before I lost count.

We enjoyed expanding once again in the sheer bigness of the state university, where I taught as an associate professor of education and drafted doctoral exams. My experience as dean of students proved most helpful.

I was about to soak up experience in still another area. Though my students were polite and friendly people, tension at Ole Miss often hung thick in the air. The discontent was not over thwarted panty raids or shorn beards.

The first black students had entered Ole Miss just a few years earlier, and racial feelings were continually reaching the flashpoint. Donna and I soon realized how sheltered from black-white strife our lives had been. We were, frankly, naive. Yet we were also Christians who believed that any hatred between people was a cancer.

In my innocence I turned to the best equalizer I knew: sports. If skill and teamwork were paramount, I reasoned, race would fade in importance.

We took a risk. Through the Presbyterian church we were attending, we began to recruit black players for an integrated summer softball team. So far as I know, ours was the first mixed softball team in Oxford.

We played nervously at first! Yet, by the end of the summer, players and audiences had relaxed and the innovation was accepted. A small step toward understanding, maybe—except for those of us who lived it and saw it happen.

With the Mississippi summer lying damp and heavy on us, I was sorry to leave the air-conditioned room where I was supervising a doctoral exam to take a call. I nearly dropped the phone. It was my former boss at MSU, a Mississippian, John Truitt—now vice-president of student affairs at Indiana State University.

John's question was simple: Would I consider coming to work with the president of ISU? Alan Rankin was searching for an assistant and had turned the recruiting job over to John, who had thought of me.

The responsibility of the post made my heart beat faster—but not with dread. I made the trip to Terre Haute and came away convinced we should accept the offer.

You'll want to know how I knew—what convinced me. I may not be able to give an entirely satisfactory answer, except that I *knew*. I sensed the initiation of peace, the beginnings of assurance that the move was right.

Complete peace (I've discovered since) may not come until I've been on a job for a year or more. That was what happened at ISU. Yet when John first made the offer to me, it felt right.

But what would I say to Donna? We had been in Mississippi only a year, and moving from Santa Barbara had been traumatic enough. Now to pick up and leave *again*—how would I justify it? What would I tell her?

My anxieties, as usual, were wasted energy. Donna also thought I was ready for more weight on my shoulders, and she was all for our going to Indiana.

Things were happening fast. A few years earlier I'd been committed to becoming a preacher; now I was number two man to a university president, set up in an impressive office suite, surrounded by intellectualism and academic power. I had never been this close to the people who make the big decisions for a great university. It was stimulating.

Still believing that I should have a ministry to these

higher-ups of academia, but concerned that I might neglect it, I jumped in and witnessed to all who would hold still. Frequently I stuck my foot in my mouth. I was the original eager beaver.

But why should I hestitate? God had entrusted to me the spiritual welfare of ISU's administrators; their souls were in my hands. I was there to save them. Why else would He have put me among such important people? They would make, after all, a set of trophies the Lord and I could be proud of, I piously reasoned.

"You know, Dr. Herron, I read that book every night when nobody's here, and it's really helped me out."

I glanced up from an eye-torturing sheet of figures. Had that voice come from the cleaning lady? What book?

It was very late. I normally did not encounter the elderly woman who cleaned Dr. Rankin's offices, but tonight I was straining to finish some work. I was mildly irritated that she'd interrupted me and that she'd read anything on my desk.

"What book? Where?" I'd forgotten her name.

"*That* one." She pointed to a copy of *My Utmost For His Highest* by Oswald Chambers; I'd kept it there intending to read it regularly, which I hadn't. Was she saying that she had?

"You mean you've been reading Oswald Chambers? Every night?" I still couldn't recall the lady's name. *She can't understand that book*, I thought, *she's obviously barely educated; no—uneducated.* Yet here she was, admitting she searched books in empty offices at night looking for answers.

I didn't know what to say to her. "That's nice," I groped. She was already sitting down, picking up the volume. Her calloused fingers turned page after page of the Englishman's profound, terse spiritual writings; *she should start with something simpler*, I thought. Then she found what she was looking for. "Dr. Herron, I wanted to ask you about this right here—I don't understand it. What's it mean?"

For an hour we talked about Christian truths, the cleaning lady and I, hunting for answers to her queries about God's forgiveness and mercy. She was not as simple as I'd thought! Sometimes I had trouble phrasing my replies so she could grasp them (had "educationese" crept into even my talk about my faith?); other times I had no answers at all, but that didn't frighten me as it would have a few years earlier.

We agreed to trust God to fill in the blanks for her, and I promised to think further about her questions and talk again. As she finished dusting the office, I could see a new radiance in her face. Then she shut the door behind her and left me alone to think.

What a crazy situation. What was I doing having spiritual discussions with a cleaning lady? I was an executive, an educator, number two to the university president. I associated daily with important people. I had nothing in common with the maintenance staff!

Nothing—except my humanity, and in this case a spiritual quest and a love for God. In Christ, occupation and social standing are cancelled out; all of us are equal. I was ashamed that I could imagine a cleaning lady's place to be lower on God's ladder than mine. She was as loved and cherished by Him as I was, and she had the same access to the King.

Who was I to dictate which class of person I should influence? Who was I to pick and choose the people who needed me? Only my ego would try to tell me I had that right; the Lord certainly had not given me that right. Here was another instance of the wind of the Spirit blowing where it wills.

I was embarrassed. Somehow I had the wisdom to turn my embarrassment into positive action: I began looking for openings to tell *anyone* about Christ, without being fussy over their status in man's eyes.

Donna and a group of other women began a Bible study in Terre Haute. Through their prayers and work, it mushroomed to eventually include 185 people! Later it became an arm of Bible Study Fellowship (after which it had been patterned). New converts turned to Christ; vital, gut-level prayers were answered.

Meanwhile, I was also growing professionally. The ISU president ran a fast-paced operation; I owe largely to Alan Rankin my present ability to keep twelve things perking in my mind at once. More and more I had to depend on the Holy Spirit, God's presence with me, to provide the energy and direction and patience I needed to carry out all my responsibilities.

There was more to having faith on the job (I discovered) than witnessing to the people I worked with; there were ethical questions, decisions to be made—choices between the morally good and the merely convenient. Later I'll be saying more about coping with cuts at my Christian standards. For now, let me say that I opened up my work to my faith, and my faith to my work; gradually the two compartments of my life lost their separateness and meshed with one another.

It's not that I worshipped my work or let its pressures reshape the foundations of my faith. I mean I saw—at last—that what I *believe* should profoundly affect what I *do* professionally—how I go about my work, not simply what I say as I do it.

7

Ultimate Responsibility

The way my career was advancing, it was obvious I would eventually have the opportunity to be a college or university president. Tentative offers began to come after I had been Alan Rankin's assistant for two years. There were inquiries from several state schools; I also heard from the presidential search committee at Greenville College, a Free Methodist liberal-arts college in southern Illinois.

Greenville sounded interesting, but so did the big universities. Here was that Christian-or-secular-education conflict back again. The knot still wasn't untied for me.

I nearly longed for my old attitude that would have dictated "Christian college or no college at all!" Now my personal growth had brought the new pain of options. Since I could serve in either place, I would have to decide for myself which way to go. Each offer that arrived, whether it was from a secular or Christian school, had to be weighed and evaluated on its own merits.

I went to be interviewed for a state college presidency; the meeting was set up in another city rather than on campus, which I had never visited. Unversed in presidential interview procedure, I was surprised to learn that—from a field of eleven candidates—the committee planned to pick a president *that day*.

They gave me reason to hope I'd be the one. Things looked good. Then, when they insisted on a commitment of five years, I balked. I had not even visited the school yet. I didn't know enough about the situation to say "yes" to that length of time. The invitation was withdrawn and I went back to Terre Haute, somewhat miffed, to report the outcome to Donna.

Maybe I should have promised them five years, I chastised myself; even if the job hadn't turned out to my liking, I could have stuck it out solely for the experience. At the time, however—confronted with the choice—I had been unable to voice a commitment that I didn't mean.

"Just remember," Donna soothed my disappointment, "You don't always *know* when God's guiding you. He must have led you to keep your mouth shut, as much as if He'd led you to say yes to their offer."

That made sense. Maybe I hadn't blown it after all. Together we began to look at other possibilities, and again Greenville appeared.

I knew Greenville College had recently gone through difficult times. Illness had forced Glenn Richardson to give up the presidency a year earlier, and the school was being headed by the executive vice-president, George Ford, until a new leader could be found. Student and faculty morale had been low because of the uncertain situation.

There were also heavy financial needs. I reminded myself

that the Indiana state legislature was benevolent toward ISU, knowing they held a public trust to keep the state universities running. This would be different. Greenville depended on private support, and the Free Methodists were not a large denomination, though they were generous toward education.

The difficulties beckoned me, daring me to try my hand at solving them. At 36, I would be GC's second youngest president. I was intrigued by the chance to fill the top spot at a Christian college, a place where I could help faith and learning work freely together—as we'd seen happening in our two other experiences with Christian schools.

Wheaton and Westmont, however, had been independent institutions, not attached to any particular church. Donna wondered whether my uninhibited style of administration would fit with Free Methodist traditions. I had no qualms about that, and I admit I did not listen to her counsel.

Later I saw that her sixth sense should have been trusted. I would say to any decision-making man that if your wife walks with the Lord, be doubly sensitive to her opinions. She may see something to which (in your impulsiveness) you are blind.

In my convocation address, my first talk to the college as a whole—for I accepted the Greenville presidency in 1970—I tried to express my desire to cross denominational boundaries. I said that I proclaimed Christianity with Christ as Lord, rather than "churchianity" with the church at the center.

I learned through that experience to be more cautious. Until people understood my motives and my style, statements I made were subject to misunderstanding. Since I had never been involved in a denominationally affiliated college, I didn't realize how deeply church loyalties and sensitivities ran. Subsequent complaints made my takeoff at GC somewhat turbulent. Still, I was flying!

When I first looked around, Greenville kids appeared radically different from those at the university. Even Westmont was liberal by comparison. Dress and hair codes gave GC students a conservative look; were they really as demure and tame as their skirt length and hairstyles indicated? At first I thought so. In fact, at times the atmosphere seemed almost monastic.

I was wrong. Getting better acquainted with the students, I uncovered the same emotions and needs and fears as in students anywhere. They were young and they were trying to cope with living on their own. Despite the college restrictions, most were more "on their own" than they had ever been.

They faced all the adjustment problems of university students, *plus* many of them were committed Christians fighting the internal battles of a deepening spiritual life, struggling to surrender to God and find the way to their true identities in Christ.

I couldn't see what the dress code, nor many of the other regulations, had to do with all this; to me, most of the college rules were superficialities, springing more from the comfort of old habit than from critical examination. Soon I found that other administrators felt the same way—that emphasis on externals was harmful. We tried to develop a more realistic perspective and a more positive campus mood, without throwing away modesty. Blue jeans blossomed among the junipers and brick walks.

New to the presidency of a college, I had a lot to learn. Second-hand and next-door experience, though they'd been helpful, were not the same as the real thing.

Eventually I found out how easily presidents can receive "purified" information. There are filters of rosy optimism and filters of self-protection and filters of "trying to save the president time." For whatever reason, the facts can come in prescreened. It took me about eighteen months to develop a more conscientious, analytical approach toward finding out what I ought to know. I had to reach a balance between snooping around everywhere and swallowing every casual rumor. Someplace between eternal optimism and hard-headed skepticism, through many errors, I began to find my spot.

Though the college had no facilities for football, I played basketball and jogged as often as I could. At Homecoming we instituted the "President's Run." In the crisp air, competitors bounced, bounded, plodded, and limped over one-to-ten miles of road bordered with red and gold leaves.

Our family loved Greenville. It was an old town crowded with trees and historic homes, ringed by woods and farmland. A short walk from campus, the town square enclosed the county courthouse. The schools were good, and people welcomed us warmly.

At first we lived (again!) in a residence hall. The trustees wanted to build a new home for us; but when I looked at the proposed cost, it appeared that renovating one of Greenville's old homes would be wiser. The college bought the rambling white brick home that had belonged to Walter A. Joy, a graduate of the class of 1900 and a true man of God. Right next to campus, the 140-year-old house became a glowing, gracious home for us and our many guests.

Donna had a profound effect on people in the community. She made friends easily, reaching out with warmth to those who were hurting. She was a relaxed, unpretentious, fantastic hostess; though she gives much credit to the example of Mrs. Rankin at ISU, I know Donna's hospitality came naturally. I felt that my approachable manner put people at ease, but I watched her make guests feel almost a part of the family. It's not enough to say the college kids accepted her; they loved her.

Though the students appreciated the historic Joy House, "oldness" was not the most popular concept at the college just then. It was late, but GC was catching up with the protest movement nationwide. Some accused the school of silence on the important issues; faculty and administration were out of touch with real life, they said. "Shouldn't Christians be in the front lines fighting for justice and opposing the waste of human life in any guise?" they asked.

I heard what the kids were saying, and I knew that for my faith to have any credibility, my world had to stay larger than the campus.

As speaking invitations came my way, I tried to accept the less traditional and predictable ones. Everyone expected the college president to speak to Christian fellowship groups; I concentrated on civic organizations, such as Jaycees and Kiwanis, the American Legion's Boys' State, political gatherings, high school graduations, the annual meeting of the utility company.

I soon discovered that the GC president held a respected post; when he talked, people listened. And because I could not speak about civil responsibilities or the college or myself without stressing the power and reality of God in us, my talks almost always included an explanation of how to trust in Jesus Christ as Lord and know Him personally.

Many people (even in that conservative and outwardly religious community) had never heard the simple gospel before; it thrilled me when they came up afterward or wrote me saying they finally understood what it meant to be a Christian. Twelve years after I had abandoned the ministry, I was "preaching" after all—not merely from the pulpit, but from lecterns in smoky meeting halls or at long tables littered with remnants of chicken dinners.

Meanwhile, Sunday after Sunday (and in innumerable counseling situations) GC students were nourished on the spiritual insight of Dr. Donald Bastian, pastor of the college church. To doubters and wobblers, and even to believers who had never thought deeply about their faith, Don showed concisely that Christianity made sense.

And it was a good thing, because a situation was coming for which logic and sense were necessities.

About the time we arrived in Greenville, a nationwide religious revival was rising among youth. A good number of "Jesus people" arrived in our student body. These kids had come to the Lord from almost literally pagan backgrounds. Through them I got a new outlook on college regulations.

These kids who had led truly unfettered lives *appreciated* the limits GC laid down for them; unused to controlling themselves, they needed external boundaries until their self-discipline was in shape. I had never seriously thought about college rules from that angle.

Yet there was another element on campus: A group of intellectually gifted kids, raised in strong Christian homes, who were simply tired of being told how to behave. They expressed resentment and anger toward the administration for cramping their style. Continually they appealed to their "freedom in Christ," while flouting college standards.

I was torn. "Man looks on the outside," they were saying, "but God looks on the inside and judges our hearts." How well I knew the principle from 1 Samuel 16:7; I had frequently quoted it myself during the beard controversy at Westmont.

But something different was going on here. Many of the

students trampling the rules still talked mostly about the *rules*, not about Christ; it was obvious their chief goal was to avoid personal restriction rather than to honor the Lord. True, of course, God judges the heart; but I wondered whether they should re-examine their real motives for resisting the rules.

Meanwhile I was fighting to change some restrictions that I found unnecessarily narrow; the administration was often one jump ahead of the students, leading even the campus reformers in radical re-evaluation of policy! There were no simplistic answers.

The end of the Vietnam war brought a marked change in student mood. Much of the tenseness evaporated; principles and respect for life were abruptly less important. I didn't think the new relaxation was entirely healthy. We tried to keep alive the spark of thoughtful criticism and the concern for higher issues.

As I mentioned before, I made some mistakes. I noticed that the "hang loose, accept me as I am" approach that we had fostered was starting to backfire; many students who expected to be met with tolerance and understanding failed to treat more conservative faculty the same way. We caught the lesson: A push for a freer atmosphere can warp into the worst sort of rigid intolerance.

The Christian college environment is decidedly unique, and it is not for all people; it is not even for all types of Christians. But GC'ers had chosen this milieu, and we did our best to give them a campus based on love, trust, and responsibility.

In no way am I implying that our efforts created something out of nothing. Greenville College had been stoking the fires of Christian liberal-arts education for nearly a hundred years; we reshaped and built on what was already there before us.

ULTIMATE RESPONSIBILITY

One autumn our small-town life was disrupted: I took a leave of absence to serve in Washington as national director of the Educators for the Reelection of the President.

For me this was the fulfillment of a vision, though I have rarely mentioned it to anyone before. I believed the Lord had shown me that I would be in Washington filling a position of influence. When the campaign opportunity came up, I didn't think about it very long; I jumped at it.

The practical working-out of the assignment proved tough and could have played havoc with our family harmony. We considered moving to D.C., but decided familiar surroundings would keep life more stable. Donna and our children remained in Greenville, and every weekend I commuted.

Other administrators took over the bulk of my college responsibilities, but matters needing presidential decisions arose continually while I was away. So I wound up doing two jobs at once and went to each exhausted from the other. The arrangement drained my physical and emotional strength. I learned the loneliness of the traveling salesman during those three-and-a-half months, enduring the unending diet of restaurant food and functioning in strange places alone.

I called home every day. I had a WATS line. If that had not been available, I would have written every day, but the phone was far better. Hearing each other's voices kept us in touch with reality and kept our relationships current. Unless you've been in a similar position, you cannot understand how I looked forward to those calls. They were my outlet for daily concerns, news, and love.

Our weekend time was too precious to waste, so we planned it carefully. We made our few hours together *count*.

Recently a woman executive told me she and her husband planned to take some "long weekends," and I misunderstood her; I thought she said "*love* weekends." The more I thought about it, the better my mistake sounded. Forced into foreshortened times together, our family learned during the campaign to live the speeding hours with intensity and joy.

On Friday, Donna would pick me up at the airport in St. Louis, an hour's drive from home; we could rely on that time alone together. I never let anyone else meet my plane. Then, after I saw Jill, Morgan, and Mark, we would do things that involved everyone in the family. Decisions on activities were made in advance so we would not consume weekend time on "What do you want to do?" "I don't care; what do *you* want to do?"

Saturday mornings had to be spent in the college offices, but I stretched my time by having college staff drive me back to the airport Sunday night or Monday morning.

Once I brought the family back to Washington with me. For a week they had first-hand experience of my life there. It helped them understand more fully what I was doing; and what refreshment it brought me not to be *apart* from them that week.

Amazingly, the leave of absence was not death to our family life. In fact, it brought us together in the determination to make the short-term assignment work. Most of all, the campaign experience wore away my false images of myself. I found out that—despite my drive to go places and see things happen—at heart I am a family man, and there would be no changing it.

8

The Prophet Motive

On a cold, crystalline blue morning in Greenville, the phone rang at Joy House. It was Glenn Heck. He was teaching now in the graduate school at America's oldest private elementary-teachers college, National College of Education, located in elm-sheltered Evanston, just north of Chicago.

Glenn and I traded notes about our families, our jobs, the record-breaking cold. Then he dropped his bomb. "The NCE president is leaving," he said, "and, Orley, the Lord showed me this morning that you'll be the next president of National College."

I had sensed something was up, but I hadn't expected a divine oracle concerning my career. "Glenn, you know I can't do anything like that. I'm under contract here to Greenville.

Besides, my field is higher education, not elementary ed. You'd better think again."

"Well, you think again, too. And pray about it."

I hung up, suddenly uneasy. Frightened. Why do Christians do these things to each other? He could have said "I think;" "I believe;" "my judgment indicates." No, he had said, "The Lord showed me."

Well, I'd learned not to blindly accept anybody's direct revelations from God. The Lord may have told Glenn, but He hadn't said anything to *me* yet, and I would need some pretty weighty confirmations before I'd consider leaving Greenville.

I told Donna about the call. She was stunned. Though we'd sometimes felt confined at GC and had fought our battles with the church over some issues, we were not looking for any way out. My seven years of college presidency had been a success: Greenville had won excellent accreditation, the financial situation was reversed, my confidence as an executive had doubled.

And our children were enamored with their schools. They were also surrounded by dozens of caring "aunts and uncles" who solicitously looked after their welfare.

Other offers had been extended to me; none of them had been tempting, and I had turned them down immediately. I tried to do the same with National College. To my annoyance, it wouldn't come unglued from my mind.

We liked where we were! Didn't the Lord want us to remain where we were happy? Of course He did. He had always led us through our contentment. His will satisfied us; we were satisfied now. That meant we were in His will. Why think of moving?

Of course God had surprised us before; several times He had opened a door in an unexpected place where we'd never dreamed a door existed. We didn't want to set our jaws, dig in our heels, and say "no!" if He was actually nudging us toward a new blessing.

Yet how could moving at this point possibly be a blessing?

If we left now, we'd be abandoning Greenville College just when mood, finances, and academics were at a peak. It would be a setback to the school; it would seem a rejection of everything I'd worked to build up. What would it look like—my walking out on what I'd done?

There was another possibility, however: We were *too* settled in Greenville; things had gone *too* well; we were resting on our successes. I had accomplished most of what I'd set out to accomplish; praise was coming to me; I was riding on momentum. Was I getting professionally lazy?

Well, what was wrong with meeting goals and then staying around to enjoy the fruits of your work? Would God be such a killjoy as to deny us that pleasure?

Maybe moving had simply been easier when we were younger. We had hit forty, and age was tying iron weights to our feet. Maybe that was why we held back.

I voiced my turmoil to Glenn at the St. Louis airport when he flew in to meet with me. For several hours we talked about National College; despite my "not a chance" attitude, I found my curiosity rising and I had a lot of questions to ask. The appeal of secular responsibility teased me, as it always had.

When I heard that National was in a tight financial spot and its atmosphere was less than buoyant, my guard went back up. It sounded like Greenville all over again—*without* the commonality of Christian team spirit. I wanted no part of that. I wasn't ready for it. Besides, in attempting to be National's savior I might deal a body blow to GC.

Glenn showed me the ego supporting some of my fears. Did I really believe Greenville couldn't exist without me? It had been standing there for a long time before I came. Under my leadership there had been solid advances; why was I afraid they'd collapse if I walked out? Was I the one holding them up, or could God send in someone else?

After all, if the Lord let anything fall, it didn't deserve to stand in the first place. "Orley," Glenn said, "God won't sink one ship to save another. He cares about Greenville, and if He takes you out of it, He's got somebody else to fill the gap." The notion of my expendability was both deflating and relieving.

There are such things as prophets, and I believe Glenn acted as one at that moment. He announced God's message to me—not assuming authority or pulling rank, but simply telling me "this is the word for you."

It was hard for me to sort out that word. People were always giving me advice, every day, sometimes seemingly every minute. If I took it all in, I'd capsize. I could barely stand to hear any more. And now here was somebody else saying, "This is what you should do."

But something made me listen this time. I trusted Glenn's character and his sensitivity to the Lord. I knew he wouldn't lie to me; furthermore, I believed his spiritual receivers were clear enough to bring in God's message ungarbled. And he was telling me, "Here's what God is saying."

I had to listen to my own heart as well; if the Holy Spirit agreed with the insight of my friend, it was certain that here was divine guidance.

As I approached the garage at Joy House, I braked to gaze across College Avenue at the snowy campus and thought an unprecedented thought: *Maybe God brought me here, not for*

Greenville's sake, but for mine. I know He's doing a work in the college; is He also–by moving me on–doing a work in me?

We asked several close friends to pray intensely for us. Through the weeks—quite likely as a result of their prayers—something new slid into our field of vision. In sermons and conversation and reading, a parade of Bible personalities began to assemble before us: people for whom obeying God had meant upheaval, opposition, *pain.*

Joseph was thrown into prison when he refused to commit adultery. Abraham had to pack up his family, his belongings, his everything and go off to an unknown land; later he had to be willing to sacrifice his own son. Moses suffered through the continual griping of the people he was trying to lead to freedom. Esther had to risk her life to expose a plot against the Jews. Jeremiah was ridiculed, beaten, and put in stocks for giving God's warning. Hosea was commanded to marry a harlot and endure her repeated unfaithfulness. Mary and Joseph appeared to the doubting public to have had a shotgun wedding. And of course Christ Himself met death by torture for following God's will.

There is no *easy* peace guaranteed with obedience to the Lord; His plans often carry heartache with them. That's how it was in Bible times and that's how it still works today. One principle was clear: God always would give us the strength to go through any circumstance. He would not leave us empty-handed, unequipped to deal with the challenge.

In our walk with the Lord we had trod on relatively smooth paths; we had naturally *enjoyed* every place He took us. What if He worked with us differently this time? What if He thought we were ready for something bigger?

"Follow the will of God and you'll be happy!"—we had heard that countless times. The promise of problem-free living, the easy way of obedience. There was one difficulty: The axiom wasn't completely true. Following God totally called for a refinement of character, the cleansing away of pride, self-seeking or stubbornness. Jesus called it "pruning," cutting off undesirable growth. If there was no pain and everything ambled along smoothly, how could the pruning occur?

"Follow the will of God and you'll stretch your faith!"—that was a better saying. Or "Follow the will of God and you'll learn what it means to depend on Him!" A line from a hymn gave us comfort, a paraphrase of Isaiah and Peter: "The fire shall not hurt thee; I only design thy dross to consume, and thy gold to refine."

I know now what I didn't know then: For a driver and an achiever, success brings a crisis. I had bounded up the rungs of my profession and grabbed an enviable batch of plums. I was president of a college, racking up good marks. What was the use of moving laterally to another college and accumulating more good marks? Besides, what if I bombed at National?

The chairman of the NCE search committee called me; I told him that under my contract I could not apply for any other position. In order to go, I would have to ask the Board of Trustees to release me from the contract. The search committee persisted. I decided it was time to notify the chairman and vice-chairman of our Board that I was considering—however feebly—the National College presidency.

Our kids still balked at the idea. Jill took it best; she would be starting college at Wheaton in the fall, and our living on the North Shore would put her only an hour from home. The boys, however, were not happy about leaving. Mark was in junior high and Morgan was about to enter high school. After spending their lives in small schools, they disliked the prospect of being lost in a big suburban system. They didn't want to leave their friends and leave everything our church offered young people.

In July the NCE presidency was formally offered to me. I gathered my staff together and asked for their honest opinions: What were the advantages and disadvantages of my leaving Greenville now? Responses were mixed. Some were sure I should stay; others saw reasons for my moving on, particularly to a place of influence in secular education. I had dreamed of a staff consensus that would settle the question for me; I got none. It was back in my lap.

Glenn Heck's judgment still counted heavily with me, although his revelation was not the bolt from the blue that he had at first made it sound. For several weeks after the former NCE president's resignation, Glenn had combed a list of possible replacements and brought National's future to the Lord. His final conviction was that I was the person. I wished I could be so sure.

We were being pressed for a decision. I didn't want to keep the committee waiting, but I wasn't ready to turn them down.

Finally, desperately, I spent an entire night in prayer. At the end of the vigil I emerged with two assurances: The Lord wanted us to go to National College, and He would provide all the strength we needed to handle what we met there.

It was not a decision of convenience or expediency. How often I'd heard people testify that they were making a move and knew it was right because God had worked out all the details in advance. There were dozens of details facing us, a myriad of impossibilities. When Jesus called His disciples, it wasn't convenient for them either; but they went, casting off security.

I do not mean to be maudlin, but you should know that I

wept over that decision. It was made against my will—or rather my hard, cold will overrode all my natural wants. Never before had I shed any tears over a move. Erased from my mind were the possibilities and opportunities that had made the job tantalizing; all its appeal was stripped away and gone. I knew only that in obedience to God I had to leave Greenville, and I did not want to go.

In late August we moved to Evanston.

9

Between Two Boundaries

National College of Education nestles so cozily on the Evanston-Wilmette line that postmen for the two towns debate who should deliver our mail. Often I feel equally pressed between two boundaries. How much should I allow students and staff to live their own lives? How much should I talk to them about my faith and personal ethics?

You may say: "Of course you have to let people make their own choices; of course you must also tell them what you believe." But trying to do both means carrying an address in two communities: the Christian life and the world.

The typical executive has one task: to be the best executive he can be. The Christian executive has that task plus another: to integrate professional competence with his faith. Through my handling responsibility the best I can, the Lord has something to accomplish in my character and something to say to the people around me.

Most Christians would agree with me in theory, but sometimes in practical specifics the idea breaks down. What does Jesus Christ *actually* have to do with the president's office of a secular, private college? Is my witness limited to putting a Bible on my desk? Or are there hundreds of opportunities to live the Christian way in the executive setting, if only I'll look for them and discover them?

You've been with me in this book long enough to know my answer: There are thousands of opportunities, everywhere! Remember what we talked about in the first chapter? Many secular jobs are filled by Christians who fail to see themselves as ministers. I believe they are unnecessarily discouraged. *Any* Christian *anywhere* has a ministry! Otherwise God has benched some people, letting their muscles atrophy from lack of action. He has work to do, both in us and in the world; since His activity never stops, neither should our participation in it.

I'm convinced that the snag lies in a misunderstanding of ministry. (You'll recall I misunderstood it for quite a while.) To minister to someone is not to cram your criticisms down his throat; neither is it to silently watch his self-destruction. To minister is not to bombard with the Bible; neither is it to hold biblical truth back from people unfamiliar with it. To minister is not to manipulate; neither is it to blandly tolerate.

What a parade of "nots." Is that going to help you grasp what your work for God should be? Realize that there are probably spider webs of *mistaken* ideas you need to clear away before you can perceive true ministry. I have spent the past twenty years sweeping out prior conceptions and bringing in new ones, reordering my ideas of what I'm doing *for* and *with* God in this world.

In my initial speech to the NCE faculty in the fall of 1977, I said that as president I planned to make decisions on three bases: (1) What is best professionally? (2) What is best for National College? And, (3) how does the kingdom of God bear influence on the decision?

After seven years on a Free Methodist campus, "kingdom of God" sounded kind of pale; but I was feeling my way. The response was affirming. Since then I have been increasingly vocal about more specific beliefs.

I met personally with each member of the administrative team to explain my professional style and personal commitments. Yet my witness must be more (so much more) than the words I say. It's how I accomplish my professional tasks, the way I treat people, my response to criticism, my accessibility to staff and students, my social behavior, and my family life. It is *all* on display.

A college president, or any executive, is never allowed the luxury of a casual comment. The words you say are quotable and taken literally, whether spoken in a closed-door policy meeting, at the swimming pool, or in the shopping mall. Whatever you say, somebody will read something into it, and somebody will tell somebody else that you said it. In the same way, you're not allowed a casual, private act; no matter where you are or what you do, *you are visible*—somebody will see what you do.

That may sound like paranoia. But I'm talking from experience and my experience has been unbelievable! There is a vulnerability that comes built-in with the job; and if you have a deep personal commitment of faith, you are vulnerable all the way down to your heart.

It is tough, this business of being a Christian in charge of an un-Christian place. The buck stops with me. Every day new issues rise: "How am I to handle *this* one, knowing what I know, believing what I believe?"

National College is a place of ministry because here we're engaged in "*growing people*." I am trying to temper one of society's prevailing winds: the teachers of small children. NCE students, now in their formative young-adult years, will teach children at an even more formative age. The power of elementary-teacher influence is indisputable. What an opportunity to mold the *teachers* first, nudging them toward a professionally competent, warmly personal approach to children—and, hopefully, also toward a commitment to Christ.

There was a time I thought my only hope for "ministry" in a place such as NCE would be starting a staff Bible study. That's an obvious move, easy to rush into. But wait. The *obvious* is not always the healthiest. God's unlimited imagination can show you ways of ministry hidden from your natural wits. Anyone can do the obvious, the possible; God deals in the unpredictable and impossible.

Now that I've said that, let me add that I *have* started a staff Bible study at National College. It began at the prompting of another administrator after my first semester here. In the beginning I led the study; now someone else usually leads. The group meets on Wednesday mornings from 8:00 to 8:30 in the president's lounge next to my office.

In no sense is attendance mandatory for staff, nor do we ask people for a weekly commitment. We feel a warm oneness as people from all religious backgrounds join in study and prayer. The freedom in praying has amazed me. Though no one is compelled to pray out loud, most mornings everyone does. Some of the needs voiced are for college concerns, others more personal. Of course we share blessings and answered prayers, too.

I'm glad now that we waited several months before beginning the Wednesday fellowship. I first worked at establishing personal trust and friendship with my staff; otherwise the Bible study could have started with a stiff, judgmental aura.

Self-righteousness lurks in the wings of any Christian's life, springing onto stage as soon as we congratulate ourselves for our fine performances. And our associates instantly spot its intrusion.

How can I stand up for my beliefs without stiffening into rigor mortis? How can I be flexible without becoming flaccid?

There is no getting around it: My moral standards differ from those of the people I'm with every day. I could try to ignore that or grind my teeth but say nothing or try to lecture my associates into reforming their lives. Clashes will come, however, despite my efforts to overlook differences. Clamming up only angers me, and being pushy makes people wonder who I think I am. There must be better ways of handling questionable behavior.

As president of a college, I am responsible for maintaining business and academic practices that are ethically pure. I could never in good conscience permit falsification of records, embezzlement, slander of a staff member, financial irresponsibility, or false claims about the college.

Do those sins appear clear-cut, easy to identify? They can get alarmingly fuzzy. For instance, I would not fire a faculty member or expel a student on trumped-up charges; but do I allow gossip and half-truths about that same person behind my office doors? I would order the rewriting of a blatantly untrue promotional brochure; but do I overinflate the college's good points when I talk to prospective students? I would clamp down on sexual irresponsibility in the dorms; but do I fire a staff member who's an unabashed adulterer?

Those are hypothetical cases, but they are quite typical of what you meet if you're a Christian executive. Let me give you a rule that may look unrealistic in print, but it has worked for me in practical experience: *You are responsible* for keeping shady practices out of your business; *you are not responsible* for enforcing your morals on employees' personal lives.

What's the distinction? It's this: You were hired to run an effective business, not to reform everyone around you. You have the right to monitor school or corporation activity; you do not have the right to control your associates' private actions.

I can hear you protesting. Sure, the company hired you to handle business—but God has also "hired" you, hasn't He? He's enlisted you to stand up for Him and His ways; His ways undeniably touch moral behavior.

True, very true. But executive authority is not a hunting license to gun down the people with whom you disagree.

Of course God dealt harshly with sin at His own Son's death; but now He deals harshly only with the stubbornly unrepentant. We must be constantly careful that in "standing up for Christ" any hardness or arrogance on our part is not as harmful as the sins we claim to oppose.

You *must* keep the channels of friendship open even as you let people know—gently—that you disapprove of what they are doing. Otherwise you project the image of a God who is unloving and intolerant, rather than the God we know, one who is patient and always ready to forgive. His rain falls on the just and the unjust; He is kind to the ungrateful and the selfish. God will never ask us to do what He does not do Himself, and the most casual glance at the world reveals that He has not yet obligated Himself to annihilate all sin.

We can only be glad and relieved that He works this way. If all error were crushed, would *we* escape? This leads to another point: Setting an example of Christian virtue means something very different from being tight and cautious, covering up every crumb of your own bad behavior.

God is perfect; but since you are not God, you are not perfect. You should be exhibiting personal growth, reliance on Him, and the assurance of His forgiveness.

Flawless behavior? If you could accomplish that, you would have never needed the mercy of Christ in the first place! Better to be honest and tell someone, "I'm struggling with that sin, too, but God is helping me out"; than to say "Who, me? I've never even been tempted to do *that*!"

What a relief! No longer do I have to conceal all anxiety for fear of "ruining my witness." I know the rumbling train of thought that thunders through the Christian mind: "I'm worried about something; I know I should be trusting God about it; non-Christians must be shown that God is trustworthy; therefore I'd better protect His reputation and put up a brave front!"

Your witness is far more credible when you admit your fears and your struggles. Why? Because then the non-Christian sees that your God is one who welcomes honesty: He's an approachable, believable, *trustworthy* God.

For years I heard that my chief responsibility as a Christian was to let my friends know "I don't drink; I don't smoke; I don't gamble; I don't go to bad movies." Now it so happens that I *don't* do those things. A cocktail party was held for us when we came to NCE; only one other person abstained the entire evening, a devout Christian Scientist. Yet our turning down liquor hardly constituted our total stand for Christ.

In fact, how is His life-changing power displayed by my avoiding things I would naturally avoid *anyway*? When I refrain from something that doesn't tempt me, what's the victory in that? I believe I'd be a teetotaler whether I were a Christian or not, simply because drinking doesn't appeal to me; refraining feels more comfortable and healthy.

There *is* a temptation that accompanies drinking, but it's a temptation that emerges in guises other than alcohol. Social drinking is omnipresent on Lake Michigan's wealthy North Shore; and though people no longer insist that I imbibe, there's the far more subtle *internal* pressure of feeling different or excluded or left behind. Thus, like a weakling, I could drink to gain approval. Everyone wants to be liked and accepted; people tolerate me now, sure, but they might open the *inner circle* to me if I shared their liquor.

Let me emphasize, this temptation doesn't always come bourbon-soaked. *Anything* I do purely to win people's favor undercuts my integrity and dishonors the Lord.

Incidentally, Donna and I sometimes go to parties and see Christians take a drink. Not all evangelicals believe the Bible teaches total abstinence, though it clearly does condemn drunkenness.

Of course (thinking of those Greenville and Westmont experiences) the final test is the attitude of the heart. Does Christian drinking carry a gnostic streak of exclusive enlightenment, special initiation? Believers who want to throw off restrictions (no matter how ridiculous or unfounded they are) must ask themselves if they are acting in true freedom or in slavery to smug self-righteousness. The obligation to *break* the rules can shackle us as firmly as the obligation to keep them.

I have given to the poor, fed the hungry, clothed those in

need; by doing these kindnesses I have tried to follow in the Lord's steps. In executive offices, however, I do not meet people in rags or suffering from starvation (at least not physically).

Here the poverty is more subtle. It is buried deeper and is harder to see. And just as a malnourished child cannot be force-fed steak and baked Alaska, a hurting colleague must always and forever be treated with tender hands.

Because we care, we won't unfailingly act in sugar-sweetness. There is a mercy that springs out of love, and there is a "mercy" that oozes out of professional laziness. We must take time to listen and develop a deep understanding of people—an understanding that tells us when to be gentle and when to be firm.

Because you're an executive and carry influence, there are people who automatically consider themselves your friends. You cannot hope to please them. They want something from you—you know it and they know it—and they cannot be happy unless you give in. Conflict is inevitable in these cases. Your job is to decide whether to let yourself be used or to stick to your professional guns.

Ninety-nine percent of all U.S. Christians know nothing about persecution for their faith. Most of us have it soft. You get a taste of persecution when on the job you come up against someone who is bitter toward you because he is hardened against the gospel. If people resent God, they will resent believers in God, and they will call up all the cattiness and cruelty they can muster.

Understand me, it will be a *socially acceptable* cruelty and cattiness. It will be subtle and calculating. You aren't dealing with dummies! You're up against competent thinking people who know how to convince and persuade. They will play the devil's advocate—sometimes more the devil than the advocate.

Remember that Jesus put up with this continually. Like Him, we can only leave our reputations in the hands of God (who knows the truth about us) and trust Him to put the right words on our lips. As 1 Peter 4:19 says, "Therefore let those who suffer according to God's will do right and entrust their souls to a faithful Creator" (RSV).

When I have conflicts with anyone on the job, I do my best (and that's not easy) to look at the situation objectively. I may be personally hurt and my ego may be threatened, but nothing will be accomplished until I pull my attention away from that and force myself to see facts.

What's important is to find a resolution of the conflict through which individuals and the college emerge as unscathed as possible. Frequently I rely on my experience with similar problems; often I ask other people for counsel. There are times I can do nothing except go on in prayer.

Plentiful criticism and confrontation is the price I pay for my administrative style. which encourages openness and frank expression of opinion. I like to ask people what they think.

Since I want an open, above-board administration, I have to search for open, above-board people. Of course we also want creative people who do their jobs intelligently and take initiative. Riding close herd on dozens of staffers is not how I want to spend my time. The executive who runs everything by himself only advertises his insecurity. A far greater credit to the college is a staff of responsible administrators who need no whip cracking over their heads.

I like to say that I'm grooming people who can take over my job *yesterday!* I want the next crop of National College leaders to be better than the present ones—myself included. It's possible for an institution to outgrow its own executives. We have to keep in touch with the whole organization and constantly develop new talent.

Let me say some things about interviewing prospective employees. I've been on both ends of the process and can suggest four guidelines that are very important:

1. You must be prepared. Study the person's credentials carefully. I look for people who have been happy in their previous positions, because they will tend to be happy here. Dissatisfied people may stay chronically dissatisfied even after they change jobs.

2. Follow up on recommendations. People don't ask others to recommend them unless they're sure the report will be good. Written recommendations often have a "halo" effect. Go beyond these canned recommendations and get in touch with the references by phone and talk with them personally.

3. Make sure you're aware of your feelings the day of the interview. No matter how well prepared you are, a hectic morning or a late night or an irritating problem can cloud your judgment. Don't superimpose your tenseness or tiredness on the person you're trying to evaluate.

4. Trust your inspired intuition. There is a *divine common sense* that many Christians don't appropriate. When I've made poor judgments in hiring, I can trace them back to ignoring that common sense. Psalm 37:6 says that if you commit your way to the Lord, "he shall bring forth thy righteousness as the light, and thy judgment as the noonday" (KJV). And that goes not only for hiring, but for every decision you have to make.

At National College I have not always obeyed my impulse to gather fellow believers around me. This is tricky. As brothers and sisters in Christ we are instructed to help each other out;

and through my position I've been able to also give others a chance to be salt and light here. But if I exclusively hired Christians, capable though they might be, I would be discriminating against those who don't share my beliefs.

No one gave me the right to turn NCE into a Christian college! I hope I've never favored a believer over someone else who was professionally better qualified. Yet I must keep guard constantly to insure fair hiring.

I have another bias, too; former athletes make great executives. I confess I lean toward hiring people who have a background in athletics. There's a reason for my tendency. Athletes are conditioned to analyze mistakes and correct them; they aren't crushed by errors, but get up and try a different strategy. Also, they are used to mapping out attacks on a problem—having a "game plan." In addition (especially if they've concentrated on team sports) they don't build an empire around themselves, but think and act as part of a team working together for one goal.

Sometimes, for any number of reasons—ineptitude, unethical actions, or simply a lack of funds for a salary—a person has to be let go. I can't tell you how to fire someone painlessly, because I don't think it's possible. But there are ways to ease the blow and soothe the hurt.

The American Association of University Professors has published accepted guidelines for terminating teachers when it has to be done. I stick to professional standards by following these carefully.

In the case of administrators and staff, we are left to our own judgment. They should be given adequate notice—from two weeks for secretarial staff (in an area where good secretarial jobs are plentiful) to nine months for administrators. I never give a termination notice on Friday.

Why not fire on Friday? Because I don't want the person to face the weekend in despondency. Let him receive the word on Monday when he'll be shored up by his colleagues.

If the person is under contract, we of course make sure every stipulation of his agreement is fulfilled. And frequently we have helped relocate former employees; no matter what the reason for firing, they deserve to find other work and support themselves.

Unless there is some dramatic infringement of the rules, firing should be *a process and not a surprise*. People who are proving less than competent should have a probationary period and continued evaluation. They deserve some solid objectives and the opportunity to change.

Here's what I ask myself: If I had to be terminated, how would I want to be treated? The Golden Rule works in this area of executive life, too.

Fortunately, staff conflicts are rare for me. Staff members almost always become my friends. I like an administration that has a structured chain of command yet is a team sharing each other's hurts and joys. My relationships may be closest with those who believe in Christ, but fellow administrators and I have always developed strong ties. We are not merely performing our jobs before each other; we are working together, understanding and respecting each other, striving for the same goals.

Here is where the president of a Christian college has the advantage. It's easier to call your staff to a deeper commitment to the college if they are already committed to the faith it stands for. Colleges naturally foster loyalty, but dedication can remain superficial if it's to the institution alone. When I say in a cabinet meeting "Let's all pray about this," a few know I really mean it; most interpret my words as wishful thinking! I say it anyway. And when I talk to alumni—Christians or not—I ask them to pray for me.

10

Pressure: How to Face It

Much of my time must be consumed in fund raising, whether I like it or not. I enjoy traveling and meeting people, and their generosity is a joy.

I've learned that personal visits are far more effective than the telephone. Face-to-face, the fund raiser can be more warmly persuasive; yet he's also more transparent, his motives more easily detected.

When I visit a person to request a financial gift, it is pointless to pretend I'm there for some other reason. I know I'm there to ask him for his money, and *he* knows I'm there to ask him for his money. An inordinate amount of politenesses, and word games, sizing-up, and side-stepping may surround the process—not to mention outright lies and bribery if they're allowed to happen. But at the core, moneyraising is extracting money from people who have it to give.

The pressures are unbelievable. I am tempted to exaggerate, flatter, and promise what I can't deliver. I am beckoned by the ruthless maxim that *the end justifies the means, or its even more seductive version that though the end shouldn't justify the means, it will this time, if I can only get this person to respond.*

Since you have probably never needed to raise a million dollars, you are no doubt wondering, "How can such mercenary thoughts tempt a good Christian?" Let me tell you, when you are held responsible for the success of a college, and you walk through its halls and see young people giving up money-earning years of their lives to teach children, and then you get on a plane to visit a millionaire who could easily donate new buildings or underwrite several more faculty members—you land at the airport with dollar signs glowing in your eyes!

I'm not implying that fund raising *must* equal blood-letting. When we need a sizable gift for the college, we don't bother to approach people who can't afford it; we approach the people who *can* afford it. If I could, I would cover the costs of National's needy students myself; since I can't, and since I know people who can, I go to them and give them the opportunity to help. Jesus taught that giving to others brings joy. Our souls are blessed when we alleviate someone else's need.

Yes, there are people who actually have so much money that they literally do not know what to do with it. We tap some of those resources for the training of excellent teachers. Money that might have gone for more temporary things is channeled ultimately into the lives of young children.

Thank God also for the people who can't afford it and give anyway, uncoerced! All giving is sacrificial; but for some of National College's friends the sacrifice is more extreme.

Whether for fund raising or some other purpose, trips sap my energy. The strain of traveling and meeting new people, the pressure of "Will they respond?" and the weight of failure if they don't, the constant mindwork, all send me back home drained.

For the person who must make repeated decisions, tiredness sounds a red alert. It's time to pull up when I feel my judgment stumbling over my own exhaustion. The real hazard yawns when I *don't* realize how tired I am; then I easily can push myself beyond my physical and mental limits.

Insensitivity to *me* means insensitivity to others. When I drive myself, I drive the people around me. No matter how knotty or desperate a problem is, the hour comes when work will get us no further; we are spinning our wheels and will be better off taking a rest. But if I don't tune in to my tiredness (or the tiredness of everyone else) I can run on the automatic pilot of an exhausted "high." Decisions made in such lightheadedness are invariably regretted.

When I return from a rapid-paced trip and must go straight into a college business meeting, I feel distracted and insecure. I need a time-cushion of rest and reflection before I leap back into leadership. That takes thoughtful travel planning; hurried trips thrown together at the last minute turn quickly to chaos, and you are forced to hit the ground running when you return.

Don't lay guilt on yourself if in the midst of a trip you abruptly get irritated with the new faces. Work out a way to take time for yourself. Carefully planned travel includes time to be alone. Though I'm a "people" person and enjoy being with others, the saturation point comes. Too bad for me—and the people around me—when I don't recognize it early enough.

A college president soon discovers that if he doesn't lead

his constituency, they'll lead him. A president must say "follow me" and then be worth following. He must also maintain close, regular communication with the chairman of the board and with the representatives of the various constituencies, such as the alumni and faculty associations.

Be careful that you don't let other people speak for you when you should be speaking for yourself. It's all too easy to abdicate responsibility and cover your tracks by letting others do your talking. Your board members are very likely the heads of their own companies, and a president likes to talk to another president face-to-face.

Take the offensive. If you are always having to make excuses for yourself, you can't lead anyone anywhere. When you're always on defense you can never gain any ground!

I avoid a lot of anxiety by *anticipating* problems and conflicts. I think through the seventh or eighth step down the line that could possibly occur. At NCE we are trying to maintain the long-range view necessary to prepare us for the future.

The chairman of our board of trustees, Robert C. Keck, is an impeccable example of *leadership*—someone who holds deep convictions and lives them out realistically. I've found that people can be led only to the degree they want to be led; and the executive's task is to lead them *beyond* that point and instill in them the desire to follow further.

That's the difference between allowing mediocrity or encouraging excellence. Some executives let their staff members do only enough to get by; the true leader prods and coaxes them to give more than they're used to giving, and more than they thought they could give.

Sometimes as I rush through an airport, the rub of the

suitcase handle reminds me I still bear a scar on my hand from tackling a violence-bent student demonstrator during one of the MSU disturbances. Other times a burning leaf-pile looks like the innocuous start of the fire that threatened Westmont.

Unpleasant as those encounters were, I often wish the enemies of my spirit were as visible, touchable, easily identified as a riot or a forest fire!

Some people imagine their temptations fading in the face of spiritual growth. Much as I wish it were true, my experience is the opposite. The longer and closer I walk with the Lord, the larger temptations loom—not the temptations to commit fleshly sins, but the temptation to *stop* walking with the Lord and start depending on my own spiritual maturity.

Amazing, isn't it? Pride flows so deep that it prevents me even from admitting my pride, let alone admitting my pride's consequences! Though it's very difficult for me to confess this, my attitude often is "I'd better take care of this problem; I'll handle it better than God can." (Of course I would never *say* that; but in *practice* my choice soon becomes obvious.)

There's a common misconception that we're always tempted at our weak points. I am starting to see it differently. When Christ was tempted by Satan, He was tempted at His *strengths*—the allure was to do what He *could* do, at the wrong time or for the wrong reason.

Remember, Satan didn't tantalize Jesus with hot-from-the-oven homemade bread; he told Jesus to make His own and feed Himself. Satan didn't say, "Jump off the temple and I will catch you"; he said, "The angels will catch you since You're the Son of God!" He didn't tell Jesus to worship him because the world was owned by hell; he said, "I'll give You these kingdoms; they can be Yours."

Jesus *could* have turned stones into bread; but even more

vital than bread was the truth of God's Word. He *could* have called angels to help Him escape death; but it was the wrong time for flamboyant miracles. The kingdoms of the world *would* all be His, but not yet—not until His earthly mission was done.

The devil is not so foolish as to tempt us to do what we *can't* do; that might drive us to the Lord for assistance. It's the Lord, after all, who wants us to attempt the impossible with Him. No, Satan tempts us at our abilities, our strengths, our talents, what we *can* do. Tricked into thinking we no longer need God, we cast off our dependence and trust our own devices.

When I face an impossible day, I am compelled to ask God for help; but when I face an undemanding day, I feel smugly secure, well-equipped, and God's aid almost seems like interference. "Today is turning out just like I want it, Lord, so come back tomorrow when I need You!" This produces a deadly delusion: Now I don't need help; I can handle it, because I'm strong enough.

I am a great one for giving things to the Lord, and a great one for taking them back again. He must have to exercise infinite patience over my continual swapping. Unfortunately (for me), as soon as I grab, *He* lets go; He hands over the controls when I insist on having them. Then I am left to cope by myself, until I figure out (again) that He can run things much better than I.

Why do I continually do this? Why must I crowd into the driver's seat when He has already proved—over and over—how much wiser and stronger He is?

I think it's because I fear the *results* of God's full authority over me. If He does the driving, He may not go where I want to go. Or He may get there sooner than I want or not soon enough. Simply put, His plans may not be mine.

Specifically, He may not bring me the personal recognition I desire. All the Bible's talk about rewards and crowns in heaven is small comfort to someone with eyes on earthly fame. It's a battle I fight every day; and if you don't recognize it, perhaps you have surrendered to your own flag and aren't even trying to give your controls back to the Lord.

When I write of God's care through the years or His guidance in my everyday life at NCE, let me be specific about what I mean.

As I have observed them, executives make decisions on one of three bases: (1) We may be faced with plain hard facts that call for an obvious course of action. (2) We may do what previous experience has shown to be wise and effective. (3) Or, rarely, we may act on blind intuition, by "feel." All three methods have their risks, and none is guaranteed to work.

I must be careful in what I say next to avoid projecting an elite spirituality. As a person who by choice has become a Christian, I have access to another decision-making resource besides those three. I believe in an all-knowing God who can enlighten my intuition and give me wisdom to act *in spite of* the facts before me and *contrary to* my previous experience. Because of the Holy Spirit's guidance, I've become a risk-taking person and life is exciting! I can step out ahead of more timid colleagues who have only their own minds or experience to rely on.

Not that I lower my horns and charge at every impossibility that waves a red flag. But I am learning to know when God *is* guiding me, and I am learning to trust His judgment more than my own wits.

My record isn't perfect. I have ignored or misread His inner leading and been sorry for it. However, I also have made decisions that I knew were right, ones that *looked* bad and like failures for a while. But in the months and years that followed, the truth prevailed and their wisdom was vindicated. God knew what He was doing all along.

Being a Christian does not mean living by mystical inner voices, ignoring external realities. I don't mean to paint that picture. God obviously communicates *through* facts and experience; sometimes they are enough. When they aren't, when something more daring and innovative must be done, a Christian can draw on the wisdom of his Father.

The Bible, of course, is with us as an objective source for both principles and examples of living God's way. When I am confronted with choices on the job, I try to examine them. Then I attempt to determine whether one course of action is encouraged by the Scriptures, or whether another is contrary to their spirit or expressly forbidden.

Naturally to *use* my Bible I must take time to *know* my Bible. The Holy Scriptures, brimming with practical advice on the ethics of daily living, reward the careful reader with comfort, support, and guidance. They cannot fail to help you decide what to do.

Am I saying you can expect God to take a special interest in the daily workings of your business? Yes, not because He prefers you to your competitors, but because if you're His child, He takes a special interest in *you* and in the things that concern you.

In the executive world we're extremely conscious of ranks and levels of achievement. We notice the marks of success. We size up a man by the dimensions of his office, the car he drives, his clothes, how many people he has as subordinates, the expense that went into his office decor. We can even be intimidated by the number of buttons on his phone.

But God has a different standard. He made all things and has all power, so He is not impressed with wealth or influence. He is impressed only with our reliance on Him, our willingness to trust Him enough to listen and obey.

Of course my unbelieving colleagues are put off if I blab about my "inner light," as though I had some exclusive celestial hot-line wired for me only. No matter how cautious I am, some offense is inevitable. Always the doubting mind interprets talk of closeness with God as boasting instead of sharing.

Though I believe God will *talk with* any person who listens, He has promised to *give His Spirit of wisdom* only to His children—people who have entrusted themselves into His family, people who have been reborn in Christ. Let me say a word about establishing such a relationship with Jesus Christ.

We all have our methods of coping with our wrongdoings. We give them free rein or try to make up for them or try to outmaneuver them by our own wits, or merely ignore them as unfortunate but unfixable.

Jesus provided another way, an ingeniously different way, when He sacrificed *His* perfect life for *our* sins. That was something no other person could do. By God's intent, Christ was the one to carry the punishment *for* us; that's what the title "Christ" actually means, an anointed or specially chosen one.

The way to God is open now for those who drop their own devices and receive the gift of His Son. Regardless of circumstances or social standing, regardless of the height of one's respectability or the depth of one's fall, Christ offers forgiveness and new life to people who turn from their own ways of coping and trust Him.

Maybe you have been told or have read somewhere that Christian faith is an emotional escape (chiefly for women?) or an avoidance of life as it is. I've talked with many who believe exactly that. I dare you to open your mind wider and think again!

Have you mentally ruled out a truth because you don't want it to be true, because it doesn't fit your closed universe, or because you don't want to face its implications for your life-style? If you have, then you are the one guilty of taking an emotional escape route—saying no without giving the matter a fair hearing.

Look at Christ again; ask Him to reveal and relate Himself to you. But remember, He is not obligated to fit your assumptions of what Deity "ought" to be. Always and forever He obeys the orders of the Godhead—the Father, Himself, and the Holy Spirit—as with one voice they are given.

And if, to find Him, you must see some entangling sins or some cherished presuppositions shattered (as I have)—know that in their place will stand the King: strong, cleansing, wise, loving, and willing to be your friend.

11

All in the Family

Our yellow Oldsmobile Vista Cruiser sped down the street, with me behind the wheel, and Mark, then six, beside me. My thoughts were on our destination; my eyes were bolted to the winding stretch of street that lay ahead. As I slalomed through an "S" curve, Mark turned to me and wailed: "Daddy, don't go so fast; I can't see any robins!"

Mark's complaint became a family classic. But for me, personally, his words were quite piercing. That day in the car I began to examine my fast-paced, large-purposed life.

Ironically, though I can't forget Mark's comment, I can't remember where we were going in such a hurry when he said it. What could have been so important to me that I kept my son from seeing a robin? What other pleasures was he missing (were we *both* missing) in my preoccupation? I had to admit, I had not been seeing any robins either.

Were my children missing the robins? Was *I* missing the robins? *Was I missing my children?* The possibility drove me to explore a place that's a tight fit for any man—inside myself.

A true introspection comes hard; it is costly. That's why it is also rare. For all our obsession with self—finding ourselves, self-acceptance, self-worth, self-image—authentic self-*understanding* still is akin to gold dust.

To observe and admire and analyze myself is not necessarily to *know* myself. I can gaze forever but never come to grips with my own ego, fears, and pride. But that's what I've had to do; and this book is part of my coming to grips.

How grateful I am that God has not left me to work out my life alone. With devastating frankness my family brings me up short when I'm foolishly plunging ahead: "Why did you do that, Daddy?" "Orley, did you mean to say what you said?"

I *need* that mirror in front of me; so does every father. David wrote in Psalm 101:2, ". . . I will walk within my house with a perfect heart" (KJV). He wanted to behave consistently, even behind closed doors, shut away from the eyes and ears of the outside world. (How many crude things do we refrain from doing simply because someone is standing nearby?) Like David's, my record is far from flawless, but I'm trying.

By the way, even if you aren't a husband and father, what I have to say applies in some way to anyone in the human race. Don't skip this section!

Although the wedding guests can't see it, a man walks to the altar carrying all the baggage of his past conditioning. Fervently as he imagines it, he cannot pack the good and leave the worst behind. The model of fatherhood he saw as a child (whether it was his real father or some other male figure) has impressed him indelibly, and its influence is going to be seen.

As he saw his father treat his mother, so the new husband will tend to treat his wife. As he was disciplined by his father, so he will discipline his child. He may try to alter his ways; but when he is pressed—and especially when words and reason have appeared to fail—he will revert to acting as his early years taught him to act. They trained him well.

If you'll identify and examine your earliest perceptions of fatherhood, they will help you understand your quick reactions to situations of pressure with your children. They will particularly help explain those repeated unthinking reactions that cause blowups and bring guilt in their wake. You may be responding not as yourself with your own children, but as your father with you—either replaying or trying to repair poor memories.

I am not saying that your father was a villain. I am saying that he has left a deep impression on you; and as you assume "his" role of fatherhood, any unresolved conflicts are sure to emerge at the worst time.

Listen to yourself! Are you responding as you saw your own father respond? *Or*, painfully conscious of your father's faults, are you now trying to keep yourself out of the same traps by doing everything *opposite* to what your father did? Either way your past has conquered you, just as overstrict religious rules can control both devotee and rebel. You may be meeting your children in the present, pulled by strings of the past. Unaware of your early life, your family will not understand.

Of course the past is real; its effects are not merely your imagination. The question is: Will you allow the past to manipulate the present, bending who you are and who your family thinks you are? Your family wants to recognize you, to *know* the real you.

I clearly recall the time I was first overwhelmed by this

truth that seems so obvious now. Jill was a very small baby in her crib there in the MSU residence hall. I leaned over her and said one of those nonsensical things new fathers say. Immediately her green eyes looked up at me and she gurgled in delighted response.

She knew my voice! Reassurance flooded over me with unexpected firm-footedness. I had touched her life and she had touched mine. We *knew* each other!

If only communicating were always so effortless. Remember the fumbling "Dill Doughnut" telegram that began my communication as a father? In the nineteen years since, I've tried hard to improve on my poor start. Sometimes I think I have done pretty well, and there are times I think I've fallen back to the level of Dill Doughnut.

Most messages, I've learned, come in subtler form than yellow telegrams; interpretation is usually stickier work than deciphering misspelled words. I'm talking from experience, not gauzy conjecture. As a father I *say* things simply by the way I act. My actions may even precisely contradict my words. When they do, it does not matter what I said; what I am doing drowns it out.

Heaven knows the number of times I've been tackled in my mental tracks: "Did I say *that*?" Seldom was "that" stated in words; more likely it was screamed by my actions, which have not been forgotten.

Think of Mark's plea in the yellow Olds—"Don't go so fast; I can't see any robins!" The way I was driving said only one thing to my son: Speed is more important to Daddy than the beauties of nature. And who can say his interpretation was wrong?

Once when I was reading the newspaper at the kitchen table, Donna came over and started to kiss me. I was preoccupied and did not give her an immediate response. Mark, sitting nearby, saw what was going on and ordered, "Let Mommy kiss you!" Right then it wouldn't have mattered how fervently I claimed, "Of course I love Mommy!" He had noticed my inattentiveness; my action—or lack of action—*said something* to Mark.

There was another time when Morgan was getting ready for his first Little League game. A few months earlier he had refused to play, and in our pride over his change of heart we were giving him extra attention. Meanwhile, however, Jill had been snubbed by her best friend and was suffering loneliness and rejection. Because of our preoccupation with Morgan, we didn't notice, and she was denied the comforting she needed right then. Our actions *said something positive* to Morgan; but they also *said something negative* to Jill.

So what does that have to do with you, the professional man, the executive? Just this: The pressures of your work make you particularly prone to distraction, careless promises, and thoughtlessness toward your wife and children. Seeds of misunderstanding lie ready to be watered by every offhand remark.

Each day your family observes you and draws conclusions from what you do and say. (If you are away on business, they observe your *absence* and draw conclusions.) It's taken me a while to see the gap between what I want to be true and what my actions are actually saying.

Maybe you aren't aware of what your life-style announces to your family. I'm going to suggest, from my own experience, some situations that *beg* to have meanings read into them.

When your job calls for hosting a reception or party, *do you send the children to bed early so they won't be in the way?* If you do, you can be sure they read your message loud and clear: "Some important people are coming; I can't be there; I must not be important." Or worse yet, "Dad's not proud of me and doesn't want me seen by his guests."

Of course you'd never *say* that to your children. But that's what they'll *think* you're saying; therefore that is what, ultimately, you have *said*.

When Donna and I entertain guests, which is often, we try our best to involve our children. Even when they were very young, they could help make preparations, serve, and tend to guests' hats and coats. Consequently, they know they count in our social life as well as in our private life. They know that rather than being embarrassed by them, we place full confidence in their behavior.

Maybe you have trouble placing full confidence in your children's behavior. But remember, your child will act as he thinks you expect him to act. Not as your words say you *wish* he would act, but as your responses say you *expect* him to act. That's how much he trusts your evaluation of him.

He will interpret being made invisible before guests arrive as your negative statement about his behavior (unacceptable); and he will believe you and act accordingly. On the other hand, he will interpret being involved as a positive statement (you trust him); and he will try to live up to your trust.

It was important for me to learn not to demand an adult level of social accomplishment from very young children. Let them participate as much as they are able, but don't force them past the point of enjoyment. If you do, they'll take still another negative reading: "I'm here, not because Dad's proud of me, but just because he needs an unpaid servant!"

Is it sounding familiar? Try this one on: If there are social events connected with your business, and your children could attend, *do you tell them they can't go because they wouldn't enjoy it?*

What my children enjoy and understand has frequently surprised me. Don't sweep away the possibility of a fun time for them by saying, "It's too adult for you." Rather than sparing them boredom, you may be denying them the opportunity to feel trusted in an adult world. They will come to inescapable conclusions: "It's boring to be an adult" (maybe you agree!) or "I can't go because I'm too little; I'm small so I don't count."

Do you think children's minds don't work that way? Do you think they don't draw such conclusions? Remember some of the misconceptions you held as a child. Improbable as they sound now, weren't they the logical results of your observations of things?

While you cannot guarantee the accuracy of all their assumptions, you *can* give your children data that help them know you love them, you care for them, and that they are important to you.

Since we're on the subject of misunderstandings, there's another signal a man can send up: Do you deny your wife and children the opportunity to support you by *covering up the tensions and worries of your work?* If you're in the habit of stoicism, they almost certainly sense your unspoken pain and feel shut out from the real you.

Athletics conditioned me to be stalwart, tough, a "man's man." Admission of pain or fear was not allowed. After my marriage, it was difficult for me to realize I could say "I had a rough day" and retain my manliness.

Gradually I realized that hiding my frustrations from my family did no good. Under pressure of concealment, the tension only erupted later in anger at some unrelated, insignificant matter.

I am not the president of my home, or the chairman of the board, or the chief executive. In charge, yes, but not under those titles! I am *husband* and *father*. Some executives leave their offices at 5:00 P.M., go home, and then continue to act as chief executive in the living room. But their corporate authority doesn't carry there! At home, the layers of officialdom should peel off naturally.

If your day was rotten, go ahead and admit what a bummer it was! Often I get release by simply confessing my failure to carry the weight I think I should carry. Then my family knows they're seeing the real me, and they rally around me in a way I probably don't deserve. Their love reinforces me, making me glad I gave them the chance to demonstrate it.

It takes courage for a man to admit he could not handle everything the day threw at him. He forfeits the "superman" image he'd like to project to his family. But remember, your children will come to adulthood as marked by their upbringing as you were marked by yours. If you play the game of Spartan strength in front of your children, they will do the same in front of their children—perpetuating the falseness and unhappiness "to the third and fourth generation." If you set the example of an honest man who is trying hard (though he sometimes fails), your children will respect you and most likely they will be real with their own children.

If you attempt to make your family believe you bend to no pressure, feel no pain—if you try to make *yourself* believe it—you are lying to everyone and you are all in for a big disappointment when the truth comes out. It is not a weakling who comes home and admits he needs the comfort and warmth of his family. It is a weakling who refuses to face the fact that his job is sometimes too big for him.

Stifling your tension at home carries still another threat:

You are going to find an outlet *somewhere*, and you may not choose the smartest substitute. I know more than one executive who tells everything to his secretary. It's an easy habit to drift into since she is loyal and committed to helping him succeed. As he talks to her, and as she listens and supports him, he may begin to see in her the qualities he used to see in his wife.

Imagination immediately takes over, casting the secretary in the best light and downgrading the wife as she now is. Eventually the secretary replaces the wife emotionally. Again and again I have seen an executive get a divorce to marry his secretary. She "understood" him and his wife didn't (or so he thought). Though the secretaries must share the blame, those broken marriages could have been prevented if the men had seen what was coming and had the spine to look for a safer place to leave their problems.

Encouraging your family to feel a part of your work life, sharing the weight of it with them, does *not* mean burdening them with its every pressure. On my way home in the evening I try to get in touch with my mood and work to improve it. There may be problems I can't put out of my mind, and it's absurd to pretend those tensions don't exist. But there are ways of dissipating the worst of the pressures, preventing them from eating away at me and later exploding.

Praying on the way home is a tremendous help to me. I pray specifically about the matters that are nagging me most, and I ask God to ease my worry. Try sharing with Him what's eating you; tell Him you want to be the best husband and father possible. Of course it's not a matter of giving the Lord information—He already knows every detail of your life. However, talking to Him will help in at least three ways: You will be more aware of His closeness; you will stay sensitive to the promptings of His Holy Spirit in your mind; and you will open doors for His help (for there are helps He won't force on us *until* we willingly ask).

Commuting time can be made into prayer time. Your "in-between" hours can serve a far deeper purpose than simply transporting your body to work. Turn them into spiritual mini-retreats! Even on a packed and stifling bus or train, you can be refreshingly alone with the Lord.

12

The Clock and the Calendar

You and I and all of us are living by a set of values: the things important to us, ranked (by us) in importance. We may have arrived at our values haphazardly or very purposefully. But we have them, and they show! Our actions advertise what comes first for us — as well as what comes second, what comes far down on the list, and what has not even earned a place.

Have you stopped to take a long look at what's driving you? No, not what you think *ought* to motivate you; but what *is* motivating you right now. It may explain why you are always running, why certain risks tempt you and others threaten, why you feel driven, why you shy away from some involvements and leap at others.

To some this evaluation comes naturally. To many, even those who have attained professional success, it's a foreign idea;

they have never looked long enough to discover what makes them tick.

I'm not proposing a mere exercise in self-discovery. If we were on our own in life and there were no objective moral law, we could live by any set of values we chose and never give it a second thought.

But we are not on our own; there is a God who made us, and He knows with what order of loyalties we'll be happiest. As I tried to cope with an advancing career and its mushrooming demands, I woke up to the fact that *my* values had to square with the Lord's or they were useless. Naturally, I'd always assumed my life was in God's hands and that I wanted what He wanted. But did I really? When I kept catching myself putting my career ahead of the Lord or my family, I knew something was wrong.

I backed up and took time (something that's hard on my system) to rearrange my priorities. To claim I was a Christian who believed God's Word, I decided I had to line up my actions by these four priorities:

1. The Lord
2. My wife
3. My children
4. My work

You will hear many men saying their families come before their jobs, when in practice it is obviously the other way around. The rankings can't be kept secret very long. Your children's first perceptions of you are basic and need-centered: You're there, you hold them, you love them, you respond to their wants. But as they grow up, they discover you have other things to do. The hours you are not home, you are doing something else, something that for some reason must be done for the family's survival.

They will promptly judge how important that work is to you (and how important *they* are compared with your work). You may tell your children they mean the world to you; but if your actions say something else, your words will be hollow and you'll not be trustworthy in their eyes.

How ironic! There are men who despise their "good" jobs; money, benefits, and ambition tie them in bonds they would gladly (if only they were brave enough) cast off. Even a man in that state can make his children believe he loves his work more than them; he spends so much time at it, and it obligates him so heavily.

The hazard is tailor-made for a young executive on the move who wants to succeed so he can provide a finer home, a higher standard of living, or more security for his wife and children. He may leave home before the family gets up in the morning and return after everyone is in bed at night. His intentions, admirable at first, soon narrow his focus to the *work* necessary to reach his goal, while the family for whom he is supposedly working are left to his peripheral vision.

What wife, what children, will put up with the insecurity of such an arrangement in exchange for material comforts? They may accept and use the comforts; but they will probably cope with the man's sporadic presence by leading their own separate lives. The family's relationships will be increasingly impersonal and casual. Amid the luxuries his efforts have purchased, they will meet as strangers.

"But," you may say, "isn't it my responsibility to be the breadwinner? Sure it would be nice to spend time with my family; but a man has to work hard to provide for them these days. That's how our society is, like it or not. Right?"

Well, right and wrong. True, you have a responsibility to provide for your family's needs. But constant work away from home does not insure your success as a provider. After all, one of your family's deepest needs is *you*—to know that you're around and that you care.

When you find yourself continually saying no to your family because you have said yes to your job, something must change or you are in trouble. You may be *trying* to show you love them by working long hours for their welfare; but if they read you differently (that your job is more important than they are), you are not communicating love.

The "noes" to your job will sometimes have to be firm. Early in my career I caught on that once you demonstrate leadership ability, you will be sought after. Your associates will covet your help and your approval of their plans. But stay aware of what's happening. You may foster an overdependence that lays unnecessary obligation on you and stifles talented people in lower ranks by cheating them out of opportunities to show what they can do.

Try saying no to some of those supposedly inescapable job demands. I know that's unnerving. But I will never forget a conversation with a friend who said he had finally started doing just that. He was amazed at how effortlessly others filled in for him. The organization kept running, and operations went on smoothly in his absence. It was a humbling, freeing experience.

You may be giving in to the fear that if you are not present everywhere at all times, someone will suspect you lack drive and ambition. Start paying attention to a more insidious possibility—that your family is growing away from you and you'll wake up to it too late.

If you really want to assure yourself of your sense of

responsibility, here's a test that requires guts: Examine the *real* reasons you accept all those business engagements that take you out of town or keep you after hours.

Are you removing yourself from tensions and expectations at home? Maybe life there is less than ideal, so you end up inventing opportunities to be gone. Whether consciously or unconsciously, if it is happening, you must admit it. If you don't, you are only letting your work mask your sense of incompetence. You may be trying to avoid what, one way or another, you must eventually face.

That brings us to a sensitive spot — the closest human relationship, which is the intimacy of husband and wife. What shape, honestly, is your marriage in right now?

I've already told you about my meeting Donna—how the first time I was with her I knew I would marry her. We both are sure that God's hand (even through my bumbling impulsiveness) brought us together. But I cannot impose on someone else's marriage choice the pattern God used for mine. Just as the Lord may give us job alternatives, He may give us alternatives of a life partner.

I'm sad when I see someone searching and waiting for that "one person," when all along in God's goodness various people have already been offered. It's healthy to be attracted to a number of persons and take seriously the prospects of marriage with any one of them. Maybe there are many combinations that could have been compatible. That's where our free will comes into play. You may not be sure, with a magical sureness, before you take the step of marriage. But what's important is to be committed for life once you take that step.

But what if you have already made your decision and now believe it was the wrong decision? You may be a respected community leader, successful in your work, influential in your church; yet under it all you are desperately unhappy with the person you married. Your regret gnaws at you, pursuing its destructive work and warping all your relationships. What do you do now?

Sometimes this situation is another sad result of the "one best person" philosophy. No, I don't mean you should abandon your wife and sample a few other options. I mean that even if your marriage *was* an unfortunate mistake at the time, you and the woman you married can still be compatible, if you will work at it. Saying "I missed it, she wasn't the right one" can be a cop-out. Experiment with the assumption that she can still be right for you, and that you can still be right for her.

I have had men come to me and say, "I made a mistake when I married my wife, but I'm going to live with her for the children's sake." Their homes, existing under the banner of "Make the best of a bad deal," will never enjoy the loving freedom that comes when there is complete commitment. I don't mean a commitment to suffer in silence or keep up appearances; I mean a commitment to love and care for the other persons involved. Merely occupying the same house under a silent, bitter truce hardly builds a healthy and secure atmosphere for raising children.

Then am I advocating divorce when a man and woman seem incompatible? I do not dogmatically rule it out, for Scripture does not rule it out when there has been unfaithfulness. But *divorce is never the best answer.* It is not even the simplest and easiest answer, though on the surface sometimes it appears to be.

Donna and I have talked with many couples who have let themselves get into a deep mire when a few months back, a few years back, if they had kept their eyes open, they could have avoided the swamp. When resentments are left unexpressed, when hurt feelings are left unspoken and allowed to eat at the heart, when deep desires are never verbalized and therefore ignored by the partner, the spaces for loving exchange are vacated, leaving bare holes of silence.

It may be *wordy* silence; the couple may talk and argue without end. But nothing gets said. No honestly personal opinions, feelings, or anxieties emerge.

Our family's experience in the 1972 presidential campaign taught us another side of this: Not only will *bitterness* explode if allowed to silently pile up, but *love* will also backfire when it is starved for expression. We need our running chain of phone calls, packages, letters, and silly cards to keep our affections current.

Loving exchange comes naturally to no one—not to Donna and me or to anyone else. Romanticism tells us it "just happens." Not true. It does *not* just happen. It is a skill that must be learned. Like any skill, it improves with practice. It requires less raw effort and becomes more refined (and more fun) as ability increases.

If you don't know what your wife wants or needs, ask her. If she is not accustomed to hearing you ask things like that, she may be surprised, and at first she may not know how to answer. But she will tell you. She may tell you gladly, relieved that you've expressed concern for her deepest desires. Or she may have built-up resentments and bear anger in her response. But the two of you must talk.

And *she* needs to know what *you* want; maybe you've been vague about the kind of wife you want her to be. You may find it difficult to express your feelings. But, I say it again, the two of you *must* talk. You will not get anywhere until you start to communicate. There is no limit to where you'll go, once you start to talk and listen to each other.

Yes, of course, it takes effort. She was not born understanding you, and you were not born understanding her. However, I'm willing to guarantee that verbalizing—in love, and without judgment—will radically improve your marriage.

That is why I said divorce is not really the answer; it certainly is not the *simplest* answer. I've seen years of stored-up hostility and frustration melt away in a few hours or a few days once the man and woman bared their real feelings to one another. Scars may remain, but new depths of love begin to heal long-festering wounds.

I would never recommend talking things out in an open group. But a third party can be most helpful, especially another person or another couple whom both you and your wife trust. The third party can provide objectivity, and also keep heightened tensions from exploding into futile arguments. The observer should never take over and certainly should never take sides, but should keep the couple talking and clarifying issues.

Let's talk about a specific form of husband-wife communication — sex. If our preconditioning grips us anywhere with force, it is here. Unresolved anxieties and needless inhibitions prevent many Christian couples from enjoying one another fully.

I think it is easier for a promiscuous person to decide to channel his energies toward one he loves than it is for a deeply inhibited person to become free. What irony! Christians, who ought to enjoy sex the most (because they most fully fathom its meaning and the God who made it) are sometimes most trapped by rigidity.

Let's clear something up. Problems that surface in sex are

not necessarily *sexual* problems. By that I mean, physical matters are relatively easy to resolve once mental and emotional strains are out of the way. If internal conflicts remain, no amount of improvement in technique (regardless of what the present flood of technique books promise) can ease the real difficulty.

It is not always a hesitancy to enjoy one's partner that hinders happiness in sex. It may be something more subtle—a reluctance to *enjoy being enjoyed* and surrender unconditionally to the other person's pleasure. Vulnerability always comes with loving and being loved. You must fully trust the other person who in turn fully trusts you. There are couples who literally will not undress in front of each other. It's tragic when fear, shyness, and suspicion are occupants where deepest intimacy should rule.

Do your children see you showing affection to your wife? Do they see the two of you being demonstrative in your love? Do you hug your wife, take her in your lap, kiss her, in front of your children? Or do they see what appears as only a cold arrangement of convenience?

As a father, you are your children's model of how a husband treats his wife. Your son will think, "This is how I should act with the woman I marry." Your daughter will think, "This is how men treat women." You may think your love is too private to be displayed. Privacy is great, but it can have destructive influence if your child wonders whether you ever express yourselves physically.

It's true that when your children are out among their peers or when they go to the movies or turn on the TV, they see a sexually loose and promiscuous society. But don't imagine you're counteracting that by putting tight wraps on everything *you* do. Your best strategy is to set an example of a married couple happily committed to each other, loving and enjoying each other.

Now, you will not find me espousing hard and fast rules for married lovers. I think "how-to" books can actually stifle creativity by implying "*this* is how it should be done." For instance, you may like to see your wife in an exotic nightgown; other husbands may think that it is better to see their wives in nothing at all! Those things are for you to decide. You and your wife need to do what is comfortable for both of you.

By the way, are you putting all the burden of attractiveness on your wife? Do you expect her to look fresh and beautiful at night, while you come to bed unshaven and in unmatched pajamas?

Recently I heard a husband voice this cliché: "Marriage is a 50–50 proposition." I'm afraid he meant, "I'm giving 50 percent and I hope I'm getting 50 percent from my wife." Marriage is not a 50–50 proposition. It is a 100–100 proposition—100 percent of you giving 100 percent to your wife, who in turn is giving 100 percent to you.

Please don't think I am setting up an impossible standard. Marriage is living together in down-to-earth reality, and it will do no good to erect unrealistic goals. These will only frustrate you and your wife, making both of you feel like failures. No marriage is perfect, and God expects perfection of no one. But you *are* capable of giving 100 percent of what you have, as best you can, to your partner. And you can start now!

Though I've already talked about spending time with your children, don't let me leave you with the impression that all you need to do is spend every waking minute with the kids, and everything will be just dandy. An accumulation of raw time does not guarantee harmony and understanding. Nor does your being away occasionally mean automatic disaster for your home.

Children are adaptable and resilient — far more flexible than we adults. They can roll with the extremes of physical, vocational, and financial disruptions—if they know we love them and value them.

But I also find my children startlingly sensitive to my moods. If I am with them in body but not in spirit, they know it, and my preoccupation cancels out the meaning of my presence.

My time with my children is not always collective. Each of them feels more freedom to open up and talk when we go somewhere alone. In fact, they are better able to communicate when there are no siblings around to compete for verbal attention. Singling out each child deepens even the briefest period together.

Quality time is essential. No *quantity* of time will make up for it. Yet there are ways to increase the quantity of time you spend with your family, too.

As an executive, you have to live by schedules and structured time. There's no getting around it. Conferences and consultations can't happen by accident; hours have to be set. But when the clock and the calendar compete with the children's needs, the children often are the losers.

If your schedule consistently prevents time with your family, here's a solution so obvious you may have overlooked it: *Write your family into your schedule!* And keep those appointments as rigorously as you keep any important engagements.

Often my date book is peppered with the names Donna, Mark, Morgan, and Jill. Too cold and businesslike? Not when it shows they're important enough for me to reserve a special time just for them. I know from long experience that unless I'm careful and unless I plan ahead, my schedule gets packed tight and my family gets left out. If business matters are allowed to run their natural course, I see my wife and children amazingly little.

Be creative—look for ways to make extra time for your family. If your job allows them to visit your place of work, by all means encourage them to come. It helps in at least two ways: They have the opportunity to observe you at work and understand more closely your chosen role in life, and it makes additional time for you to be together.

Of course, not every job situation allows family visits. You can hardly have small children running in and out of an operating room or a submarine or a lab full of radioactivity. But keep alert. If there is an open house at your plant or office, some event accessible to the public, let them come to look around.

I'm grateful that my work situation has never required shutting out my family. Ask my associates and they'll tell you that Donna or our children often drop by the office to ask me something or just to talk. They know the door's always open.

A good way to gain intimate time with your children is to pray with them—and I don't mean making them recite "Now I lay me down to sleep." I mean praying with and for them, out loud, and encouraging them to pray out loud, too—for themselves, for others, and (yes!) for you. In our family, the best time for prayer turns out to be before bed, when the day's distractions can be laid aside and bodies are ready for relaxation.

The prayers don't have to be long or wordy or grammatically perfect. What's important is that your child learns to be direct and open with God.

Frequently I hear myself uttering prayers for public consumption, thinking that by sounding eloquent or clever or circumspect I prove my Christian maturity. During the opening months of Lyndon Johnson's administration, the President hosted a White House luncheon and asked Bill Moyers, his press secretary and an ordained Baptist minister, to ask the blessing for the food. Moyers had the people bow their heads, and as he began to pray, he was interrupted. "Speak up," President Johnson said, "I can't hear you." Moyers replied, "I'm not talking to you."

The straightforwardness of childhood talk with God is something we should never outgrow. Once when Mark and I were praying together, he prayed something that my stereotypes did not accept as appropriate. Just as I was about to correct him, I realized he was only being honest with the Lord. If I had admonished him, "Mark, you shouldn't say things like that when you pray," I'd have been conveying a God of *distance* with whom we must be formal, polite, and semi-real. Instead, I took Mark's example and let it make my own prayers more spontaneous.

If I simply let life happen, the demands of others and my own momentum will close my family out. That's a sure thing. It is up to me to control my schedule, to "take dominion" over it as much as humanly possible. And being frantically busy does not always equal making wisest use of my time.

I constantly feel driven to "get a lot done today"—"a lot" defined as piles of tangible reports written, plans drawn up on paper, cash raised. Ridiculous. The *intangibles*—the invisible but incalculably weighty effects of an hour of privacy with a son or daughter, or a mid-afternoon phone call to my wife—are the things real life is made of. And if I plan for them, I can see to it that they happen.

13

Body Language

There are two questions I want you to answer honestly: First, how many overweight executives do you know? And second, are you one of them?

Today you may be sorry for the shape you're in. Six months from now you won't be—if you *decide*, and *act on* your decision, to do something good for your body.

If you're happy with your present condition, and proud of it, good for you—patrol it like a watchdog. Don't let it get away.

Many presently overweight executives were star athletes in college only a few years ago. They played football or basketball or soccer. They were gymnasts or milers. They trained every day. They kept themselves in great shape. Then life's focus changed; they entered careers and went into training of a different kind. Paperwork and problems with people outran the attention they gave to their bodies. Now their physical life lags behind their professional life; they fight fatigue, self-conciousness, and doubt.

Well, isn't it unavoidable? Executive life seems designed to doom physical fitness. Look at your routine. You must continually take your associates out for lunch or dinner. You linger talking over food and drink. You meet people in restaurants at odd hours, consuming unneeded extra meals ("snacks," you call them, but they're often bigger than your lunches or breakfasts). You find yourself in hotels in strange cities with nothing to do in the evening, so you go have a bite to eat or order some food sent up. Maybe you could stand all this food if you burnt it up in exercise; but, unfortunately, the main muscles you flex are the ones you use to talk, write, push elevator buttons, and hail cabs.

What can you do to help your body? How can you find time to get started, even after you make up your mind to do it?

Well, in the first place, there are other ways to confer with people besides over food. But even more than that, the principles for finding hours for your family also operate here. You have time to exercise, if you look for it.

Recently another man on our college staff had something to talk over with me. Both our schedules were tight. He said, "Why don't we go swimming this afternoon? We'll talk about it at the pool." We did! We combined exercise with ideas and came away invigorated.

Your workout times can be seminars on the move. Often when I need to talk business with someone, I ask him to play racquetball or jog or work out in the weight room with me. Of course not all sports are conducive to discussion, but a whirlpool or sauna afterward beats conferring across a desk. People are more approachable after exercise; defenses are down. And we wind up the conversation feeling great instead of tense.

Does your place of work have a pool or a gym? Use it! Is there an athletic club nearby? Join it! You can even keep an exercise bike in your office. It will say to your associates, "I care about my body and I treat it well." Some exercise bikes are so portable you can take yours with you on business trips. Or you can get an isometric exercise device to use anywhere.

Whenever you travel, try to stay at places with swimming pools. Some athletic clubs have reciprocal agreements that allow you to use clubs in other cities. Even if you don't belong to a club, many communities now have recreation facilities that stay open late at night for travelers. Think how tensions will evaporate and how well you'll sleep if you've been exercising instead of sitting and snacking in front of the TV.

You can do your body a big favor by getting an intelligent idea of which foods you can enjoy freely and which foods you should avoid. Food is continually pushed at you, but usually you have a choice between something heavy and something tasty but with fewer calories. Stock up on "safe" refreshments. Anyone who knows me knows that I consume a lot of orange juice at work, and I try to spread the sunshine by offering it to anyone who comes to the office.

What's important is not to be a prisoner of others' poor food choices or others' inactivity. Encourage the people around you to exercise with you and eat better with you, and they'll wind up thanking you for it.

Of course the first stop on the way to any new exercise or eating plan is your doctor. He can tell you what kinds of workouts are wisest for you and which foods you should eat based on your special physical needs. Even if you are disabled or handicapped in some way, your doctor can help you stretch your physical limits. The boundaries are wider than you may believe.

That also goes for thinking you're too old to start exercising. It's *not* too late to begin feeling better. Don't quit on your body. It has potential you've only imagined.

Your body is not the total you; you have a mind and a spirit trying to express themselves through physical action. Does your inner self get a fair chance? Is your body supple, responsive, and animated? Or does it communicate only your poor eating and exercise habits?

I'm not saying we should *not* be governed by habits. We should *take* control and establish *good* habits. Eating well and working out can be ingrained in your system. They can be part of your daily schedule and automatic. But they become automatic only as you consciously practice them and build new food and exercise patterns.

Don't be unrealistic and tell yourself, "Four days from now I'll have brand-new habits." You have to keep working at it, and you will probably suffer lapses. But in four days you *will* notice improvement in the way you feel and the way you look at yourself. That will encourage you to keep it up.

What about my family? Do they fit into my fitness program? By all means. Workouts make ideal family times. The exhilaration and refreshment of playing ball or running or bicycling together will break down barriers. Strong ties are formed skiing down a mountain, hiking, or canoeing together.

For instance, I recently took a business trip to an area known for good skiing. Mark went with me, and we made it a working mini-vacation. We had time to ski together and I had time for conferences as well. Get away with just your wife or just one of your children when you can; you'll let them know you like having them along, and they'll get a closer look at what you do.

You want to be a better husband, a better father, a better executive—don't you? Then start taking better care of your body! All those trite things you've heard are true (that's why they've become trite): You'll feel better, you'll look better, you'll perform better, you'll like yourself more. And you'll be more attractive to the people around you—including the wife and children you love.

14

Creative Giving

First let me warn you, if you're looking for a pat formula for handling family finances, this isn't the place to find it. I believe the Herrons' funds are handled by mutual trust and good sense rather than by unbending law.

That's not to say we treat money lightly. Cash is no casual matter with us. We have a daughter in a pre-med program in college. We have two growing sons continually outgrowing their clothes. Money counts, and we have to handle it wisely. Yet the temptation of compulsive buying beckons us all the time.

Any executive is exposed to his associates' material acquisitions—expensive objects that often have been bought primarily to set up a plush atmosphere and advertise the owner's good taste. Perhaps the buyer surrounds himself with them to prove his own importance; it's an easy step from "I have these things" to "I deserve these things." I've known people who possess fine paintings or sculpture and know nothing about them except in which country they bought them and what they cost.

Yet the visitor draws a different conclusion: Since successful people own expensive things, when *he* acquires expensive things he will be a success. So he buys. Not because he needs the things, not even because he wants them, but because of how the things (and therefore *he*) will appear to other people.

When you stop to think about it, of course, you see it's all a game. But most of us never stop to think about it. We simply go on spending, acquiring, growing bored with what we have, and spending and acquiring more. Possessions thus become only a means to please ourselves and impress the people around us.

There's a different perspective possible. For me and my family, as committed Christians, money and things are "on loan" from God. We are supposed to care for what we have, using it to support ourselves, help people in need, and widen the influence of the Word. Practical decisions must be made for carrying out those aims, but those aims are the groundwork for our spending.

How does it work? Here's what happens when I receive my paycheck: A certain percentage is given away, the scriptural ten percent for Christian ministry, plus more for other worthy causes. (This isn't a "tip" to reward God for getting us through the week; it's a grateful response for His care, plus a practical way to pay the physical expenses of the Lord's work.) Then we take what's left and decide how to use it. There may not be a large amount; but whatever there is, we want to manage it the best we can.

What I *don't* do is dictatorially dispense cash to Donna and the children, expecting them to live on my dole. Donna and I have joint checking and savings accounts. We don't think allowances are the answer to money management problems. Our children receive enough money for their daily needs, with reasonable latitude for special purchases. We are paying Jill's college expenses since she hasn't had time to work during the school year, though she picked up some money as a lifeguard last summer.

Special purchases are handled cooperatively. Our children do their share and we do our share. We help them out, but we also try to teach them to shop carefully.

Here's an example: Just last fall, Morgan received a total of one hundred dollars in birthday gift money. He had been wanting a guitar. He could have gone out and blown the whole amount on an inferior instrument. But Donna and I told him that when he had found a really good guitar, we would pay half the price if he could pay the other half. For five months he saved his money and haunted guitar shops, and last week we bought the guitar. He had kept his end of the bargain; we kept ours.

When your child says, "I want this," it's easy to give in and buy it for him without thinking. Neither of you benefits from doing it that way—your child doesn't learn anything about looking for value, and you may throw away money on something that won't last.

Consult *Consumer Reports* and any other buyers' helps you can find. Show your children how to search out better quality at better prices, how to literally get more for their money. If that's something *you* never learned to do, then learn with your children.

About eighty percent of what we own was bought at reduced price through sales and discounts. It isn't that we mind somebody's making a profit. It simply makes good sense to pay less when you can get equal quality. It's better stewardship of the money God has given you to use.

Some Christians don't tithe because they think they can't afford it. What we need to remember is that God knows about all of our needs and has promised to take care of us.

That's why I think churches should provide classes in stewardship and money management. I also believe every church needs a business manager—not merely a person who holds that title, but someone well-trained in money matters with an awareness of God's providence as well. When churches lack careful financial plans and confidence in the Lord, they wind up taking the "emergency" approach to spending—stumbling along appropriating money by guesswork and then scraping up special offerings when a big bill comes due.

In fact, by mismangement a church inadvertently pushes people onto a road as dangerous as compulsive buying — *compulsive giving.*

Of course God wants us to support mission work and give to people in need. But He also provides us with wisdom to evaluate and choose among the many possible recipients of our gifts.

Appeals strike at the emotions and impose guilt feelings on us. Be careful. There is nothing wrong with arousing sympathy for the needy; but are there also *facts* presented to support the emotion? You should have a personal knowledge, interest, and understanding of every cause that receives your money. And don't be surprised when a gift to one organization brings a flood of other requests; lists of names and addresses are frequently exchanged or sold.

I don't mean that every appeal you see is shady! You may

have to decide between several sincere and worthy causes. However, if you are pressured into giving to every one that comes along, your gifts will be spread thin. God can multiply a small gift if that's all you can give; but if you can give one *large* gift, why cut it up into tiny pieces?

I am cautioning you against unwise giving. But it isn't unwise to give! I'm against compulsive giving; but *impulsive* giving, when God prompts it, can be a beautiful experience.

And whether it is impulsive or planned, your giving will be rewarded. You cannot outgive the Lord. He loves to be generous with His children. I don't mean every Christian is automatically entitled to a mansion or a yacht. But if He knows you'll use such things wisely, if in it you'll build bridges to hurting friends who feel comfortable talking in a massive library or on a cruise, He may let you have one or both!

In fact, our family is enjoying a mansion right now. A vast and luxurious lakeside home is provided for the NCE president. We're grateful that God would entrust us with so many beautiful things, and we welcome others to share them with us.

Knowing that God will reward us, do we give with only the reward in mind? I hope not, but no person's motives are one hundred percent pure. God would not promise you a return on your gift, then expect you to forget that promise when you give! If He has promised rewards, it's no sin to anticipate His keeping His promise.

However, I've noticed something: If I give and then consciously wait for the "kickback," it does not arrive on schedule. For me the rewards come when I least expect them. They come in a way I could not predict, when I am not even looking.

While I was president of Greenville College, I was in Chicago on one of those biting, wind-blasted days only the

Windy City can produce. I walked by a store window that announced "SALE ON COATS." Grappling with my own coat against the wind, I suddenly thought of two GC students who always went around campus in light jackets. They did not own warm coats; they were from poor families and could not afford them.

On impulse I went into the store and bought two winter coats, took them back with me and gave them to the students. They weren't high-class garments—imitation leather and imitation sheepskin. But they were the first warm winter coats those young people had ever had.

It was reward enough for me to look out my office window and see one of those students crossing campus in the coat I'd bought. But after a week I had a phone call from a woman who was a friend of our family. She had a coat, she said, that she had worn only once; could Jill use it? She sent it (Jill's initials had even been sewn in) and it fit perfectly. Only a week later, the same woman called again to say she had still another coat for Jill; she sent that, too. We passed along the benefits by giving one of the coats away. But here was what spoke deeply to me: both Jill's coats were real fur. I had given away artificial hide and leather; the Lord had given back the real thing!

Another time, while I was working on my Ph.D. dissertation, I noticed that the pastor of our church wore the same suit Sunday after Sunday. I knew he was sadly underpaid. It was obvious he was not going to have another suit unless someone bought him one. He and I went to a clothing store together and when he found the suit he really wanted, I purchased it for him.

I went back to my office, and on my desk I noticed a "window" envelope. Having just spent all that money, I wasn't anxious to look at a bill, so I ignored it. After several days my secretary picked it up and opened it. "Haven't you read this yet?" she asked. "You've won a tailor-made suit!" My memory had to be jogged several times before I recalled trying out a sample pen and filling out a form. There had been a drawing and I'd won the grand prize! That tailor-made suit I eventually gave away, too.

Later I bought a blazer, slacks, shirt, and shoes for the same pastor. You may think I thought that if the suit worked, a whole outfit should work even better! But I believe I did it because he still needed clothing and we were able to help him. In a few weeks (should I have been expecting it by now?) a lady who was chairman of the board of a corporation sent us a check for $500. She knew I was working on my doctorate, she said, and thought we might be able to use the money.

You can't give more than God gives!

One Christmas season I was teaching a high school Sunday school class. I gave each of the eight kids a silver dollar and asked them to pray about how they could give it to the Lord. I was eager to hear the results of their experiment in giving, but it did not occur to me that my $8 was also a gift. On Monday morning we received an $88 bill for a small TV we had bought. Across the invoice the dealer had written "Merry Christmas—paid in full." My $8 had become $88!

Maybe I am still learning on an elementary level. Maybe I need mathematical oddities and coincidences like these to show me God is there. For whatever reason, this is how He works with me.

It's exciting to see our children taking the same attitude toward giving. I have set them up in a small jewelry business where they invest in and sell gems, and we are giving away our profits. Recently Morgan voluntarily gave his warm jacket to a boy who didn't have one. We believe the willingness of our children to give grew from the atmosphere of our attitude toward money.

If you want to launch out on a real giving adventure, here's something to try, something we're beginning to practice: When you spend extra money on a luxury item, give the same amount for Christ's work. If you can't afford to give that much, then you can't afford the luxury either.

I'm not saying you should deny yourself all pleasures. The point is that when you're about to spend money on yourself, you must ask whether it would be better spent somewhere else.

For instance, most Sundays after church we eat out together as a family. There are lots of additional nights we could do the same, but we have to ask whether we shouldn't spend the $40 or $50 some other way. Usually we decide to invest it on something more lasting.

You could say our mansion by Lake Michigan is partly illusion; we are not that rich and we have no prospects of being that rich. But we know the Father who has everything and who loves to take care of us. We enjoy what He has given us and pass it along to others, but we avoid compulsive buying and compulsive giving. A frozen financial formula? No. But it's based on solid principles of trust, love, and sharing. What better treatment could a paycheck hope to receive?

15

Handling Success

Young Elsie was taken to a recital to hear a famous soloist. The performance was magnificent, and the little girl seemed spellbound. Suddenly, in the middle of a moving song, she burst into tears and had to be taken out of the hall.

"What's wrong?" Elsie's father asked. "Don't you like the singer?"

"Yes," wept the little girl. "But I'm scared she'll make a mistake!"

That priceless story, told by Elsie Ward (an Evanston schoolteacher now in her nineties), demonstrates precisely the cost of the fear that God will do us wrong—somehow He won't understand what's best for us or His wisdom will lapse and He'll make a mistake. Our composure shatters; our enjoyment of Him is disrupted. Shaken and dubious, we are drained by our apprehensions. And in the end we miss the great performance. We fail to see what God really is doing for us.

I was raised to be a seeker of new heights and I love to succeed. That's how I'm built. For whatever reason, the things that I'm associated with usually turn out well. And continually I catch myself wanting to succeed for the sake of success—for the way it makes me feel, for the praise I get from others.

Yet God has different standards, as I've said before. Since He can do anything, success does not impress Him. Only trust wins His favor—and trust is required most in the face of failure, not success.

Why? Because when everything is going well, it takes no effort to believe God is doing things right. The track is well-oiled and faith slips along with no friction. Then a rough place comes. It's jarring. You get hurt. And you hear the mocking voices: "Look what happened! You trusted the Lord, and He let you down. He dropped you."

Rationally, of course, your theology could never admit such thoughts. The perfect God cannot make mistakes; everything He does is right. He is consistent. Yet when you follow Him and everything appears to go wrong, your true theology surfaces. Do you behave as if you're dealing with a God who's still good, or do you behave as if He's a bumbling incompetent who needs you to straighten Him out? It's your life, not your lips, that reveals the God you *actually* believe in.

I don't mean to be overly harsh, but we must get down to basics. If you doubt God's wisdom or His care for you, it's better to admit it than to cover it up with pretended piety or to play mental escape games. When my actions are challenged and I'm under pressure (wondering if following God is going to work *this* time), I'm tempted to live in either the past or the future.

"Remember how good it used to be?" "There's a new day coming—if I can only do this or go there!" I mentally try to remove myself from the situation. But it doesn't help. False comforts and false promises only incapacitate me for the present, rendering me unable to meet the conflict and carry out my work here and now.

My standards are high. When I don't perform as I think I should, I get tough on myself. And I get tough on the Lord. I'm following Him, so why doesn't He see to it that everything I do comes out right? After all, He's promised not to fail me, hasn't He?

But my responsibility is not to succeed; it is to obey. If we follow, He'll take care of keeping score. Since our move to Evanston I've seen it more clearly than ever: God's measure of success is not necessarily ours.

It's true that He won't fail us and that with our lives in His hand we'll wind up winners. But our idea of winning and God's idea of winning may not be identical. We want to succeed; He wants to raise healthy children. His way, even if the way is strewn with obstacles, is the only true road to success for each of us.

To change the metaphor, His office has no wastebaskets. He will do what is right because He is who He is, sovereign in the world and sovereign in your life since you've asked Him to be.

I find myself waking up earlier in the morning now and praying; I spend more time consciously in God's presence. I know I start doubting my call to this place when I neglect close fellowship with Him. And it's an easy step from doubting His call to doubting His ability to talk with me, and this undercuts my trust in Him.

Our family is here because we followed God here and

we're going through life by His leading. Leighton Ford reminds us that Jesus' Great Commission in Matthew 28:19,20 (usually translated "Go ye therefore, and teach all nations, baptizing them in the name of the Father, and the Son, and of the Holy Ghost: Teaching them to observe all things whatsoever I have commanded you . . ." [KJV]) should better be translated, "*As you are going*, make disciples . . . baptizing . . . teaching." In other words, *as you are making your way through life*, do these things.

Wherever God calls you is significant, because it's God's call—not the place itself—that gives you significance. And God may trust you with a highly influential position. I find myself in one of the most exciting educational institutions in America, attempting to influence the teachers who will influence our children.

The Communists say that if you give them a child until he is seven, they have a Communist for life. I want to spread the influence of Christ among as many young children as possible. And one way to do that is to "make disciples" of their teachers. We want teachers who are sensitive to the academic, social, *and* spiritual needs of their pupils.

God will hold me accountable for my leadership at NCE, just as he'll hold a pastor accountable for the leadership of his church, or the president of a Christian college accountable for the leadership of his school, or you accountable for your sphere of authority. In God's eyes there is no difference; if we're Christians, our responsibility is equally heavy. ". . . Unto whomsoever much is given, of him shall be much required." (Luke 12:48, KJV).

The years have shaped my personal goals and distilled them to two:

(1) To fulfill God's will and be conformed to His image.

Right now that means being not only a good college president, but the best college president I can be. I'm a constant student of how I can be a better executive. A leader can never retire from learning.

(2) To serve my fellow man—first my family, then others. When I see hurts, I want to soothe them in the love of Christ. I don't want people to remember me as a dynamic executive and a neglectful family man. If it came down to the choice, I'd rather be remembered as a good husband and father, though an average executive; but I believe it's possible, with the Lord's help, to excel in all our endeavors!

That's my ministry. Now I smile when some well-meaning person gushes, "You should have been a minister!" I *am* a minister. And I always have been.

The Lord has given every one of us a work and a place to belong. In the end there is no other reason for our going or staying anywhere.

And when someone asks, "Orley, what are you going to do *next*?" for the first time in my life I can truthfully say, "It's in God's hands." I don't know right now what I'll do next; I may stay here forever or I may move on one day.

But I know that if I'm always gazing into the future, I'll be little good today. I could orchestrate my future and manipulate things into being. That would be my cleverness, not God's providence. I prefer to trust Him to work things out in His way. For now, I'm here. And I like it!